# THE STARTUP CTO'S HANDBOOK

ESSENTIAL SKILLS AND BEST PRACTICES
FOR HIGH PERFORMING ENGINEERING TEAMS

## ZACH GOLDBERG

**Disclaimer:**
The publisher and the author make no representations or warranties of any kind with respect to this book or its contents, and assume no responsibility for errors, inaccuracies, omissions, or any other inconsistencies herein.

At the time of publication, the URLs displayed in this book refer to existing websites owned by the author and/or the author's affiliates. WorldChangers Media is not responsible for, nor should be deemed to endorse or recommend, these websites; nor is it responsible for any website content other than its own, or any content available on the Internet not created by WorldChangers Media.

2023, Zach Goldberg, zach@zachgoldberg.com

Paperback: 978-1-955811-56-9
Ebook: 978-1-955811-57-6
Library of Congress Control Number: 2023918702

Cover design: Michael Rehder/www.rehderandcompanie.com/
Layout and typesetting: Paul Baillie-Lane/www.pbpublishing.co.uk
Editors: Stephen Nathans-Kelly & Paul Baillie-Lane

Published by WorldChangers Media
PO Box 83, Foster, RI 02825
www.WorldChangers.Media

https://ctohb.com
https://startupctohandbook.com

To Max Mintz, for teaching me to learn and
value the important things in life.

To every direct report I've ever had, thanks for your patience
and looking past what I'm sure were my many mistakes.

To my wife, for tolerating and supporting my
many pursuits, this book included.

# PRAISE

"A foundational guide for any engineering leader!"

**Gordon Pretorius, CTO of Typeform**

"Zach's concise chapters of how-to wisdom artfully distill decades of on-the-job experience leading early-stage technical teams. Worth checking out!"

**Daniel Demetri, CEO and 3x Start-Up Executive**

"The CTO Handbook is an inspired collection of practical, actionable recommendations for aspiring and experienced technology leaders alike. Whether you're in the process of building a world-class engineering team from the ground up, have ambitions of becoming a CTO, or have been in the role for years, this handbook serves as your indispensable guide."

**Eric Johannsen, CTO at Dama Financial,
author of *C# 8.0 in a Nutshell***

"When I was stumbling around in the dark trying to figure this out for myself and overwhelmed with several tech management books, this is the concise summary of all the things I needed."

**Charlie von Metzradt, cofounder of MetricFire/Hosted Graphite**

# CONTENTS

| | |
|---|---|
| **INTRODUCTION** | **1** |
| **1 PEOPLE & CULTURE** | **9** |
| 1.1 MANAGEMENT FUNDAMENTALS | 9 |
| 1.2 HIRING AND INTERVIEWING | 49 |
| 1.3 ONBOARDING | 85 |
| 1.4 PERFORMANCE MANAGEMENT | 94 |
| 1.5 TEAM MAKEUP | 110 |
| 1.6 LEADERSHIP RESPONSIBILITIES | 119 |
| 1.7 WHICH TYPE OF STARTUP CTO ARE YOU? | 132 |
| **2 TECHNICAL TEAM MANAGEMENT** | **137** |
| 2.1 TECH CULTURE AND GENERAL PHILOSOPHY | 137 |
| 2.2 TECH DEBT | 145 |
| 2.3 TECHNOLOGY ROADMAP | 153 |
| 2.4 TECH PROCESS | 157 |
| 2.5 DEVELOPER EXPERIENCE (DX) | 171 |

## 3 TECH ARCHITECTURE 177

| | |
|---|---|
| 3.1 ARCHITECTURE | 178 |
| 3.2 TOOLS | 203 |
| 3.3 DEVOPS | 207 |
| 3.4 TESTING | 222 |
| 3.5 SOURCE CONTROL | 233 |
| 3.6 PRODUCTION ESCALATIONS | 240 |
| 3.7 IT | 244 |
| 3.8 SECURITY AND COMPLIANCE | 246 |

## 4 CONCLUSION: MEASURING SUCCESS 251
## 5 BOOK REFERENCES 253
## 6 GLOSSARY 259

## ABOUT THE AUTHOR 263
## ABOUT THE PUBLISHER 265

# INTRODUCTION

## Always Be Learning

At the age of fourteen my parents sent me to several weeks of sleepaway computer camp. It was every bit as geeky as you're picturing in your head: rows of folding tables with dozens of (mostly) young boys glued to their gray CRT monitors, paying more attention to the game Unreal Tournament than to their programming lessons. Two years later, at sixteen, I went back to computer camp as a counselor/programming teacher, and I loved every minute of it. I was very lucky that, at a young age, I recognized—and my parents supported—my love of computers and software programming.

Fast forward another few years to the summer before my freshman year at the University of Pennsylvania. I knew for sure I wanted to study computer science as an undergraduate, but I also had the idea in my head that I liked business. My father had started his own business, my brother had just graduated business school, so business seemed like a great idea. Penn is known for their dual degree programs that let students graduate with degrees in multiple fields, like engineering and business.

That prospect seemed perfect to my eighteen-year-old self, so I emailed my advisor, Dr. Max Mintz, and dutifully set up a meeting to discuss my application for the dual degree program. Being an incredibly generous and student-focused professor, Dr. Mintz graciously agreed and invited me down to Philadelphia to talk about it over a cup of coffee at Tuscany Cafe.

On the chosen day, having driven three hours from New York to Philadelphia, I sat down across from Dr. Mintz, eager to hear how to game the system. I figured it was a matter of choosing the right classes and getting sufficiently good grades to qualify. Dr Mintz, however, had other ideas.

Full of anticipation and ready to take instructions on how to polish my résumé, I took a sip of my coffee and asked him: how do I get into the dual degree program? The man I would soon come to know only as Max picked up a napkin and drew an X-Y axis on it, then looked me in the eye and asked me if I knew what special relativity was. I wish I had a video of that moment, as I imagine my face contorted into a rather amusing shape. Before I could finish my answer, Max was off to the races. For the next two hours he proceeded to introduce me to Einstein's theories. By the time we had finished, my brain was broken, and not once did we get to discuss anything about Penn's dual degree programs.

We had several more coffees over the coming months, and any time I'd ask Max about an application or a résumé, he'd steer me right back into real science. Max wanted me to *learn*—not just to absorb whatever topic he was lecturing about at the moment, but to get really good at learning, and learning hard things at that. Max couldn't care less what piece of paper his students were given at the end of their four years as long as each of them was prepared to continue learning for the rest of their lives.

By the time I graduated college, Max had become a close friend and confidant, and he had fundamentally shaped the path of my education. Rather than give me fish, Max handed me a fishing pole and taught me how to attach bait and cast a line.

No single book can give you the experience Max gave me as an undergraduate student. I make no such promises for the book you're reading now. Instead, I tell this story to emphasize the value and impact of a focus on the fundamentals of learning itself.

As a technical leader, the desire, willingness, and aptitude to continue learning are critical to your success. There is far too much tech knowledge out there for anybody to become a true expert in everything needed to work in modern technology. I like thinking of a person pursuing a career in tech as a character in an RPG game that, rather than killing enemies to level up, must spend forty hours a week at a job collecting skill points. You get to choose the skill trees on which to spend the accumulated points, but you need to choose wisely. The variety of skill trees is vast enough that it's impossible to unlock all of them, so you must specialize.

The most wonderful thing about tech is that our field is continuously evolving. The people you work with will change. The tools you use will be updated or deprecated, and new techniques for doing your work will come and go. As you embark on your adventure in technical leadership, the only way to manage this change is to expect it, accept it, and embrace the opportunity to learn and grow with your team and the field itself.

> *I want people to be serious about learning. I want them to dig in. I want them to gain, most importantly. It's not RSA, it's not [nuanced algorithms]; those aren't important. It's that confidence in themselves they can grow and learn outside of academia: that means they don't need me. All they need is to be able to sit down with books—or perhaps today the internet—and go off and learn things on their own.*
>
> Dr. Max Mintz, 1942–2022

# The Startup Technical Leader's Dilemma

Most startups have a "technical cofounder." This person writes the bulk of the initial codebase, hires the first few engineers, and runs the technical show for the startup at least through their first one or two rounds of funding.

Somewhere between hiring the third and tenth engineer, this person will stop being "hands on keyboard" and start spending all their time managing the team. At this point, problems often arise: the team begins shipping features more slowly, the defect rate begins to climb, system stability may suffer, overall costs go up, and the other founders start to worry.

Chances are the technical cofounder, or any technical leader, has spent their entire career up to this point investing their time and effort in becoming a great programmer, not into developing leadership skills. It should come as no surprise then, with their leadership skills at level 1, that they're making mistakes and costing the company time and money.

Regardless of your title and when you joined the company, if you've devoted most of your career and experience to technology and you're now assuming responsibility for people or a department, it's critical you realize that you're now in a leadership role; your technical background and talents won't be enough on their own to be successful. While some technical skills are table stakes for running a software engineering team, the reality is, to do a good job as a leader you need to focus on people leadership, management, architecture, and general decision-making skills.

People leadership isn't for everyone. I'm sure you've heard stories of technical founders who stepped aside as their companies grew. Steve Wozniak, cofounder of Apple, is perhaps the most famous example of this pattern. There's no shame in stepping aside; Wozniak recognized that technical work was what he loved, and that's where he wanted to spend his time. You'd do well to at least consider the same for yourself: decide if programming is your zone of genius and the work that gives you the most joy. If it is, you'll have a great career ahead climbing to the ranks of the most senior technical staff.

If, however, you or your circumstances have led you to conclude that managing or leading a team is the role you aspire to, then this handbook will provide a good starting point on how to broaden your skills on the journey to becoming a successful technical leader.

# The Author

I had my very first startup experience during the summer after my freshman year of college. I have no memory of why I sought out an internship at Eduware, or why they accepted my application. What I do remember is commuting every morning to work in a tiny room in the back of a first-floor office with four other young software engineers. The oldest of us must have been twenty-five; I was nineteen. It was just the five of us sitting around a horseshoe-shaped table, working shoulder to shoulder on a

.NET education application. I was probably useless as an engineer, but I was fortunate that the oldest and most senior engineer of the group took the time to teach me and help me understand the tools, and I gradually became more productive.

Something about that experience in a stuffy room at the back of the office must have left a good impression on me, as I've chosen to work at seven more startups since: Invite Media, WiFast (now Adentro), SoChat, AutoLotto, Trellis Technologies, GrowFlow, and Equi. At Invite Media, a display advertising and exchange bidding company, I partnered with the CTO to lead a rapid growth phase that culminated in its 2010 acquisition by Google for $81 million. At Google I took over site reliability responsibilities for Invite's departing CTO and oversaw the company's integration into Google's stack.

From there I went on to cofound WiFast, a tech company focused on democratizing and monetizing Wi-Fi usage, serving as both CEO and CTO through our first two major funding rounds. I've also served as Entrepreneur-in-Residence at Tencent in Guangzhou, China, and cofounded SoChat, a cross-platform messaging app. Since then, I've served as CTO at Lottery.com, Trellis Technologies, GrowFlow (acquired by Dama Financial), and Equi.

I've approached each of these roles with a "founder's mentality," working to establish creative environments and advance the idea that engineering software should be more science than art.

I've also been fortunate to learn from others throughout this journey, including seven teams of fantastic engineers, countless consulting/coaching clients, and many brilliant cofounders. I've also proactively sought to elevate my own leadership via years of management coaching from one of Silicon Valley's top coaches, as well as tapping countless mentors and reading hundreds of relevant books.

Through my reading, it's become clear to me that while there are hundreds of how-to books for programmers and people working with specific tech or tools, and dozens of helpful books for CEOs and CFOs on the financial side of entrepreneurship, one thing our industry is missing is a thorough, practical resource for startup tech leaders. We need a resource that covers all the topics in between the core skills, and addresses the range of leadership challenges and skills so critical to our role.

There are also plenty of blogs on how to write good code, or how to run user surveys, or on finding product market fit. This is a book on technical team building; it addresses all the skills a leader needs to build a company that they didn't learn in traditional tech education or experience.

# Using this Book

As a leader of a software engineering team, chances are you've encountered some of these issues in your role:

- Tracking, managing, or paying down tech debt.

- Hiring, attracting, cultivating, and retaining top talent.

- Creating an objective, fair, and transparent performance review system.

- Building, managing, and sustaining a healthy and generative company culture.

- Navigating your relationships with other leaders at your company.

- Enduring slow decision-making or endless circular arguments among technical staff about how to architect and build your system.

It would seem that every technical leader faces these issues at one time or another, and yet advice on how to handle them is inconveniently left out of nearly every business or technical curriculum.

My aim is to provide perspective on these problems and more, as well as offer context on how various techniques play out in the real world. The goal is to arm the reader with an understanding of the tradeoffs, some visibility to see around the corner, and frameworks that will prepare you to make your own well-reasoned decisions.

This book is written primarily for anybody who is presently or may in the future find themselves managing a software engineering team, particularly

INTRODUCTION

as the driving force of a venture-backed startup. It may also prove useful for individual contributors—non-manager software engineers—as a means to gain perspective into the kinds of tasks and demands placed on managers that may not be obvious at first glance.

I've formatted this book as a collection of independent chapters covering a broad spectrum of topics. It is intended to be used as a reference guide, for the reader to pick up a chapter as it becomes helpful and not necessarily read sequentially from start to finish. For this reason, some material is repeated in various chapters to ensure that each chapter can stand on its own without the benefit of the prior sections as context.

My goal in each chapter is not to provide an exhaustive discussion or review on the topic. Instead, the goal is to introduce the topic, provide an overview or a structure for thinking about it, offer some best practices, and suggest reference material to explore the subject more deeply. Think of this book as a breadth-first collection of topics related to technical leadership. It's up to the reader to determine which topics are most interesting to them, and, equipped with some context and perspective, do a deep dive on what's most relevant and put the knowledge into practice.

At the end of the day this book is a synthesis of my personal experience and the resources I've found helpful, interspersed with advice and input from peers, mentors, and advisors. If there are things in this book you disagree with or believe are incorrect that you'd like to let me know about, or if you find this book helpful and would like to communicate with me directly, feel free to reach out at zach@ctohb.com. I'm also happy to discuss advising, coaching, and mentorship opportunities at the same address.

# Business Processes

Throughout this book you'll find many descriptions of business processes. My goal in outlining these processes is to provide a starting point for how you might implement a solution to a problem you are facing.

Depending on the size of your team and company, what is described here might appear overly burdening and cumbersome, or it might seem too sparse and unsophisticated to address your needs. The reality is that, as your company and team grow, you will need to reinvent the ways you do business. Your company of five people will operate very differently when it grows to twenty or fifty or a hundred or a thousand. I've highlighted the core principles that matter and left it to you to adapt them to your team as it's constituted now, and also to scale your approach as the needs and constraints of your business change in the future.

# 1

# PEOPLE & CULTURE

## 1.1 Management Fundamentals

Recommended Reading: *Managing Humans* by Michael Lopp

The golden rule of management: do what it takes to get the best out of your team. In technical leadership as in any other leadership role, the best measure of your performance as a manager is the performance of the team itself. That means you should be thinking about and spending time doing everything necessary to help individual team members do their best work, both independently and collectively.

Helping your team succeed requires humility, as it entails consistently putting the needs of your direct reports above your own. You will need to adjust and tweak your style, behavior, thinking, and actions to suit the needs of members of your engineering team. That will include being willing to be wrong, being open-minded, and learning from your direct reports.

If you buy into this journey, know that you will make mistakes. Own those mistakes with your team and they will trust you more for it. Also know that being a perfect manager is not an achievable goal; the best you can hope for is to always be improving in small ways. After a career spent managing people, you'll have learned a lifetime of lessons about technology and human beings that will make you a more competent manager.

In *Managing Humans: Biting and Humorous Tales of a Software Engineering Manager*, Michael Lopp writes:

> *"Every single person with whom you work has a vastly different set of needs. Fulfilling these needs is one way to make them content and productive. It is your full-time job to listen to these people and mentally document how they are built. This is your most important job. I know the senior VP of engineering is telling you that hitting the date for the project is job number one, but you are not going to write the code, test the product, or document the features. The team is going to do these things, and your job is to manage the team."*

In that one succinct paragraph, Lopp hits on all the key points of management. First and foremost, you are a listener, a personal and career development coach, and a shield against external forces in the world which might distract, stress, or otherwise prevent your team from doing their best work.

## THE PROFESSIONAL SKILL TREE

Many video games involve a concept of a "skill tree." For those unfamiliar, a skill tree is a sequence of skills or abilities that are unlocked as the player progresses through the game. Each skill is unlocked by spending "skill points." Here's the rub: at any given time, there are more skills to unlock than you have skill points to spend. The skill tree forces you to choose some skills before others. The skill tree provides a reasonable model for your career as well. At any given job, you're likely accumulating skill points toward some skills and not others.

In your journey to tech leadership, you've already invested many skill points into the technical/engineering branch of the skill tree. My key insight for you is that the management branch of the skill tree is equally vast, and if you've not been investing points in that area up to now—even if you're a Level 100 engineer—you'll start your new leadership position as a Level 1 manager staring at a mighty oak tree of yet-to-be-unlocked crucial skills. Once your company has more than a small handful of engineers, these skills will make the difference in your ability to scale up with the team.

### *Kaizen*: Continuous Improvement

*Kaizen* is the Japanese word for "improvement." The phrase was popularized as part of the Toyota Production System. At Toyota, all personnel are given a (literal or metaphorical) red handle to pull that stops the entire production line. If a worker identifies a problem with production, the idea is for them to pull the red handle, gather coworkers and resources to diagnose the issue, and then resolve it before work can continue. By empowering everyone on the team to improve the process and to be invested in its efficacy, Toyota can cost-effectively build higher-quality cars.

I'm not the first to suggest that software engineering has much in common with traditional manufacturing (see *The Phoenix Project* by Gene Kim). In this case, make the metaphor real: provide your team with a digital red handle and encourage them to focus on continuously improving everything you do. Members of great teams understand that, over time, the team will change, customer requirements will change, tools will change, and the team will need to revisit past decisions and make improvements.

*Kaizen* applies not only to your team's process but also to individuals. Your best team members will embrace the idea of continuous education and continuous improvement, and treat mistakes not as failures but as opportunities for improvement.

## COACHING

Your principal role as a manager is to get the best out of the people on your team, so in many scenarios it's more appropriate to describe your role as that of a coach rather than a manager. A coach is somebody who is on your side, a source of wisdom and guidance to everyone on their team. A coach is quick to provide critical feedback, but also the first to celebrate and praise success.

Your goal in your interactions with your direct reports, whether they are individual contributing engineers or managers themselves, is to be the best coach they've ever had.

### Find a Management Mentor

One way to jumpstart your leadership transition, coaching and managing others, is to find yourself a management mentor, rather than learning by trial and error. There are a lot of management coaches out there with different approaches; the challenge is to find one that resonates with you.

In my first role as a business leader at WiFast (then Zenreach, now Adentro) we quickly hired a team of ten full-time employees, mostly in engineering. As a first-time manager I knew I had a lot to learn, and I was eager to take advantage of every resource I could to become a better manager. My only problem was I hated most management advice. I found it either overly prescriptive (do X, then Y, then Z) without context or insight, or entirely devoid of substance—"fluff," if you will. That was until I met my first management coach, Jonathan.

The story goes that one of our investors, First Round Capital, was hosting a management summit in San Francisco, about a thirty-minute drive from our office. Thus far I'd found First Round folks were high quality, so when I came across the invitation, their support temporarily muted my ever-present fluff allergy and I signed up.

When I drove up to the summit, I was encouraged that the audience was relatively small, only about thirty people—enough to fit into what felt like a high-school classroom. I sat down at the high-school folding-tray top desk, opened my notebook, took out a pen, and wrote the date and "First Round Capital Management Summit" at the top of the page. Sadly, that would be the only thing I wrote for the next four hours.

The first half of the day had three or four speakers talk about various topics, every one of them lacking in any actionable advice or insight. As we broke for lunch, I contemplated driving back early and getting in half a workday at the office. I checked the agenda and noticed an entirely different roster of afternoon speakers, so I decided I'd at least hear out the first one.

The first speaker after lunch was Jonathan. Unlike prior presenters, he had no slides and he seemed a little rushed, perhaps a tiny bit unprepared, or maybe just nervous, as he walked to the front of the class. The first words out of his mouth, however, told a different story: "Allow me to transparently manipulate you."

I'll never forget that moment. What a funny thing to say; it's a seeming contradiction in terms—like saying, "This sentence is false." (If you're curious, this is called the Liar's paradox—ctohb.com/liarsparadox.) He went on to explain that that was exactly the point: he wanted to say something to grab our attention as an audience, and at that he succeeded perfectly. For the next thirty minutes I took copious notes, not on manipulating people but on understanding people in general. I hung on every word Jonathan had to say. As the half-hour session wrapped, Jonathan said he had to catch a flight, and somewhat hurriedly ran out of the room. I looked down at my notebook, processed that I had taken three pages of notes in the last thirty minutes, then stood up from my chair and ran after him.

I managed to catch him just as he was getting into a yellow cab. Somewhat exasperated, Jonathan asked me what I wanted. I asked if he did private coaching. He replied, "Ask the summit organizers to connect us." Cleverly, he didn't commit one way or another to coaching on the spot, leaving himself the opportunity to do due diligence on me via First Round before deciding if I was worth his time. Luckily for me, when I asked First Round to put us in touch, the contact said nice enough things about me that Jonathan agreed to an introductory coaching session.

## 1:1 MEETINGS

A 1:1 meeting is a private meeting between you and a direct report. It's tempting to treat 1:1s as status check-in meetings, and for the agenda to focus entirely on business or technical topics immediately at hand. It's all right if the agenda includes those topics, but this is your opportunity to establish a coaching relationship with your direct report. You should use this time to really get to know and understand how your report thinks, draw out and identify their strengths, and recognize weaknesses you can address to help the person do their best work.

## SKIP-LEVEL MEETINGS

It's good practice, on a semi-regular basis (monthly or quarterly), to have meetings with the direct reports of any managers that report to you. These are called "skip-level" meetings as you're skipping over a level on the organization chart by meeting with them directly. You're not trying to undermine your managers with skip-levels—in fact, it's quite the opposite. By collecting more data and hearing different perspectives, you'll be better able to work with managers on things that can help improve the business.

Some quick thoughts for agendas of skip-level meetings:

- Put the employee at ease by making sure they know the purpose of the meeting—that you're not there to problem-solve or make decisions that are better handled by their actual manager.

- Let them know that you want to build a relationship and hear their insights on leadership, culture, strategy, and company direction.

- Connect with the employee; ask questions and get curious.

There are many good actual templates/agendas for skip-levels on the internet. Here's one from managementcenter.org that I recommend: ctohb. com/skip.

## COACHING MANAGERS

As your organization grows, you'll likely get to the point where you no longer have any individual contributor direct reports. Every direct contributor who actually writes code is managed by a middle manager. It should be obvious, then, that effective middle managers are critical to the performance of your organization. It's your job to make sure that your managers have the support, resources, training, and mentorship they need to enable them to do their best work coaching the engineers on their team.

The biggest contributor to cultivating high-quality middle management is, of course, hiring the right people, but second to that is ongoing training and support. If you're in a position to be overseeing a team of managers, I encourage you to build the following into your organization:

- Build a culture of continuous learning.

    o   For example, encourage your managers to set up an internal management-focused book club.

    o   Share insights you're learning yourself with the management team regularly, and have them do the same with their teams. If you're using a company chat tool, a dedicated channel for #management-insights or similar is a great place for this kind of dialog.

- Establish a high bar for coaching and management.

    o   Be clear with your managers about your expectations for what management means, for expectations on coaching, 1:1s, performance management, etc.

    o   Codify your management expectations unambiguously in internal documentation and make it part of management hiring and onboarding.

- Provide thorough and accessible management training materials.

    o   Supply resources for your managers to pursue ongoing learning and professional development. This might include purchasing company subscriptions to learning programs, sponsoring employees to attend conferences, hiring management coaches, or formalizing internal or external mentorship programs.

- Consider the cost for these training materials in your regular budgeting process for every member of your team.

- Develop an external-facing culture of thought leadership.

- Encourage your managers to become thought leaders in your industry. This could take the form of a company, participating as a guest on technical or management podcasts, or speaking at conferences.

## COACHING ENGINEERS

### 1:1 Meetings with Engineers

Your engineers should be venting at you regularly, so if they are, don't panic—this is totally normal, and in fact highly desirable. You should have a 1:1 meeting with every member of your team at least once every two weeks, if not weekly. Your goal in these meetings is to create a safe space for your engineers to tell you what's on their mind, and for you to actively listen and engage on these topics.

With strong engineers, that will mean they're aware of imperfections in the world around them and they want to tell you about them. Your job is not to solve every problem they bring up; your job is to listen, to ask questions to clarify your understanding, and to convince them that you do understand, and then steer them toward solutions. From time to time, there may be a direct ask, or something you can directly help with, but that's not the norm. The value you're providing here is making your direct reports feel heard and coaching them to productively handle issues themselves.

## 1:1 Content and Agenda

Ultimately, your goal in a 1:1 meeting is to build a relationship with another person and have vulnerable and critical conversations that enable you to help them do their best work. If your direct report has a broad agenda, that's great, start there. However, if their agenda is consistently limited to tactical in-progress work items and you're not getting to those higher-level how-we-work conversations, then I encourage you to supplement their agenda so they better understand the purpose of your meetings and bring more substantive concerns to future sessions.

The easiest way to bridge your agenda and theirs is to have a shared document, perhaps with some structure/template, to elicit the kinds of discussion topics you think are important. Having this document available prior to your meeting also gives you and your employee a shared place to capture ideas in between meetings, to structure thoughts in advance of a meeting, all of which help make the meeting time more productive and efficient.

There are several SaaS tools that help facilitate 1:1 conversations as well. Notable examples include Culture Amp and 15Five. You don't need a tool though; a simple document works equally well. The template I use is available at ctohb.com/templates; it includes prompts for discussing liked/wished for items at a personal, departmental, and company level, as well as bidirectional feedback between manager and employee.

## 1:1 Playbooks

Establishing a playbook for these engineering 1:1s is another useful way to make sure these meetings address a consistent set of topics and don't go off track. Your playbook should ensure that your 1:1s touch on the following:

- **Conflict:** Inside your immediate team, across engineering teams, cross-functional

- **Performance and Development:** Often it's your engineers seeking advice on how they can improve something

- **Clarity:** Engineers may have general thoughts about something and are looking for your perspective, or to see if you have different info than they do about something

- **Context:** What's going on more broadly at the company, and how does a contributor's work relate to those goals/objectives

## Radical Candor

The phrase *"Radical Candor"* was defined by Kim Scott in her book *Radical Candor.* The book defines Radical Candor as communication that incorporates both praise and criticism, and ensures that the delivery involves both "caring personally while challenging directly." I think the point is best made in contrast to three other kinds of communication outlined in Scott's book:

- **Obnoxious Aggression:** Sometimes referred to as brutal honesty or front-stabbing, characterized by direct challenge but lack of individual caring, perhaps demonstrated by insincere praise or unkind criticism
- **Ruinous Empathy:** Communication that comes from a place of caring personally but lacks a direct challenge
- **Manipulative Insincerity:** Also known as backstabbing or passive-aggressive behavior, characterized by neither caring personally nor challenging directly

I encourage you to read Scott's book, but if you don't, then at least be aware of these terms and use them as a coaching tool to move your team toward regularly practicing Radical Candor.

## BENEFITS OF OVERCOMMUNICATION

There's nothing worse for an employee than feeling like their manager doesn't communicate enough with them. In the absence of information, it's a natural instinct to assume the worst-case scenario; a lack of information can also be a prime source of anxiety and confusion.

Overcommunication, by contrast, has very few consequences. The worst that can be said of overcommunication is that it can prove a distraction or become redundant, which are problems easily remedied with a bit of thoughtfulness as to the form of overcommunication. It's no surprise, then, that most startups invest heavily in building overcommunication into their culture, often including the phrase as a company core value.

### EMAIL

Pretty much anyone you interact with nowadays has either been using email for twenty-five years, or since they were in early grade school, so of course this means they know how to use it effectively, right? Unfortunately, effective use of email at work is not necessarily common sense. So, it comes to you to help encourage best practices. Here is some general advice for using email effectively:

- Don't let email become your job.

    ○ Rather than having email open all day or monitoring it continuously, check email at fixed times each day.

    ○ Disable email notifications on your phone. Though this one in particular may seem blasphemous, I encourage you to try it. Not only does it significantly reduce the number of notifications you receive, but you'll find yourself building a new habit of proactively checking email when you're ready to engage. This makes email an intentional activity instead of a continual background nuisance.

1.1 MANAGEMENT FUNDAMENTALS

- Get to inbox zero every day.
  - Invest time in learning your email tool or use optional email assistant add-ons/plugins that help sort and triage email so that, by the end of the day, every day, you'll have zero unread emails.
  - Zeroing your inbox doesn't mean acting on or responding to every email. If you're using email as a to-do list, that's fine (though it's not ideal—see Meetings and Time Management, page 28, for better to-do list alternatives); just make sure to triage your email to-do list out of your core inbox so that you won't confuse it with untriaged emails.

- Don't problem-solve in email.
  - Email is a suboptimal medium for having an in-depth discussion, especially when more than two people are involved. Group emails are best used for coordination and overcommunication, not problem-solving.
  - Understand that email tends to lack nuance and tone of voice, which makes intent easy to misconstrue.
  - The temptation to write or participate in a nuanced group email thread is a good indicator that a synchronous conversation is a better forum for addressing the topic at hand. A fifteen-minute discussion can often resolve what an email thread of twenty messages will only scratch the surface of.
  - The act of writing down one's thoughts is often a very productive exercise, but email is not a great way to facilitate and capture that written brainstorming process. Encourage your team to instead write memos in a wiki to facilitate deep thinking.

- Don't rely on email for long or in-depth communication.
  - In general, email is a poor medium for long-form content. Long memos are better put into internal wikis or documentation that can be commented on, updated, and easily referenced in the future.

21

○ Keep emails relatively short—ideally, bulleted for key ideas. Don't hesitate to use basic formatting such as bold or highlighting for requests/action items.

- Be mindful of your audience.

    ○ Engineers in general prefer to be writing code instead of reading/answering email. Ask yourself if an email is really the right way to communicate with your audience. In general, the best method of communication with somebody is *their* preferred method, not yours.

    ○ It's very easy to leave coworkers off an email thread, either intentionally in an effort not to flood inboxes, or as an innocent mistake. If you're sitting there thinking about which people to add to/remove from an email thread, that's a good sign email is the wrong forum to begin with.

## SYNCHRONOUS CHAT

Chances are high that your company has already adopted some form of synchronous chat platform; in the early 2000s it was commonly Google Chat or an MSN messenger product, while in the 2020s it's more commonly Slack, Microsoft Teams, or Workspace from Meta. If you're not presently on one of these platforms, it's worth considering their adoption. The vast majority of companies ranging from day one startups to goliath companies of 100,000-plus have adopted them with great success.

Achieving that success means being mindful and planning around some inherent flaws: synchronous chat programs require both parties to stop what they're doing and engage, and they result in conversations that are poorly organized and do not produce lasting artifacts for your team to reference. You can and should recognize these downsides and compensate for them by setting up basic etiquette and expectations for your team in how to use these tools.

Slack's own blog includes a great article with some common best practices at ctohb.com/slack.

Here are a few recommendations for working with synchronous chat tools:

- Try to include all the necessary information in a message to continue a conversation. If you're asking a coworker a question, provide sufficient context and information in the question to give them the best chance at being able to answer comprehensively. Doing this minimizes the number of notifications sent, reduces the amount of back-and-forth communication, and shortens time to resolution. Tools like loom.com are very helpful for this.

- Use message formatting features, such as bullets and headings, to make longer messages easier to scan and relevant information easier to find.

- Centralize conversations in specific channels or threads. It's unproductive and frustrating to try to follow a conversation with multiple people on more than one topic at a time.

- Lean into notification schedules and do-not-disturb features. You should also encourage members of your team to set up a do-not-disturb schedule in any synchronous chat program to minimize interruptions in focus/flow time.

- In the spirit of overcommunication, default communication to public channels. Even better, establish a culture and standard operating procedure of turning conversations and resulting decisions into long-lived, organized documentation in the company wiki or other appropriate document/information store.

- Be extremely judicious with messages that send notifications to multiple people, e.g., @here or @channel in Slack. Especially as your company grows, the odds are that sending such a message will send a notification and interrupt potentially dozens of employees.

## ASYNCHRONOUS COMMUNICATION

Asynchronous communication is any communication that is not intended to get a response immediately. To be effective, the receiving party should be able to take their time, process the information, and then reply thoughtfully. A key element of asynchronous communication is that the initial message is a complete thought and contains the necessary context to allow the other party to respond.

A trite example is the dreaded "the feature is broken" bug report. In nearly all cases, bug reports should go to a ticketing system rather than a direct message. An engineer receiving a bug report in a message does not have the context to know which feature is broken or in what way it's failing to meet expectations. So, the reply from the engineer will likely consist of a handful of questions, requiring more round trips with the reporter, costing time and creating frustration.

Contrast that with a bug report that includes full written reproduction steps as well as a video of a user trying to use the feature and demonstrating the failure. More than likely, this approach will enable the engineer to produce a fix without requiring any further follow-up.

The bottom line is this: any time you send a message to somebody in an asynchronous format, give that person all the information they need so they can understand, process, and reply in a way that advances the conversation.


## ASYNCHRONOUS CULTURE

You'd be surprised how often well-thought-out asynchronous communication can substitute for a synchronous chat or a meeting. Not only can good asynchronous communication mean fewer meetings and interruptions, but it can also leave behind comprehensive written documentation for others to process in the future. Some startup companies, such as Levels Health, have actually built the idea of asynchronous-by-default into the core of their company culture to great effect (ctohb.com/async).

## DOCUMENTATION

Documentation is a key element of scaling up your organization. The benefits of writing things down are many: written documentation can assist in onboarding, training, overcommunication, thoughtfulness, thoroughness, building culture, avoiding unforced errors, and more. Your role is not just to believe in the value and ROI of documentation, but to build a culture of documentation and a team that values it.

Some tips for building a culture of good documentation:

- Live the value yourself and set an example for the team. Once I moved a team from writing zero internal wiki articles per week to writing several per day in the course of about eight weeks. Literally the only thing I did to encourage this cultural change was to start writing articles myself. Everything I did that made sense to share with the team I wrote up as an article, and I'd make a point of sharing links to those articles whenever appropriate. Very quickly, other managers started doing the same, and within two months everyone on the team was contributing every week.

- Build documentation—both adding to and reading from—into your process. Whether it's for onboarding, technical specifications, pull reviews, internal requests for comment (RFCs), or memos, the standard procedure should be to write it down and preserve it in an organized archive in a readily accessible location.

- Develop processes to maintain documentation where appropriate. It's easy for documentation to go stale, and in many situations that's perfectly fine. In others, it's important that documentation stays up to date, and the only way that will happen is if you have a process or checklist that includes updating the documentation. Having a "last updated date" on every document is a great way to signal to readers that something is fresh or potentially deprecated, stale, or out of date.

- Encourage the team to practice the Boy Scout Rule (always leave the campsite cleaner/code better than you found it). If they find documentation that is inaccurate, they should either update it themselves or explicitly mark the document as deprecated.

One key area of documentation you should pay special attention to is how a developer gets started writing code within a particular project or repository. I recommend every repository have a README.md file that explains a minimum of four things:

- **Installation:** How to get the application installed and running locally

- **Directory Structure:** How to find your way around this codebase

- **Development:** What the develop/run/test loop looks like on this codebase

- **Deployment:** How you get your changes into higher environments for this app

## On Acronyms at Work

Every organization has its own distinct culture, and its own style of internal and external communications. One of a leader's key responsibilities is to make sure that culture always supports the goals of the organization rather than impeding them.

One element of the internal culture of technical organization that tends to get out of hand is the generation of made-up acronyms that can multiply over time and obscure and overcomplicate the communication they were intended to streamline. This may seem like a minor annoyance, but it's symptomatic of poor communications strategy that can spiral out of control, particularly as it can place barriers between those "in the know" and team members who have no clue what the acronyms stand for. As an organization's technical leader, it's your job to set the tone and define the culture, and although the proliferation of made-up acronyms most likely won't start with you, it's your job to recognize when it's happening and shut it down before it gets out of hand.

In a January 2018 memo to SpaceX employees, Elon Musk called for a "No Acronyms" policy. I've put that same policy into practice ever since, and I wholeheartedly endorse it. The below came from an email titled "Acronyms Seriously Suck" (ctohb.com/acronyms):

"There is a creeping tendency to use made-up acronyms at SpaceX. Excessive use of made-up acronyms is a significant impediment to communication and keeping communication good as we grow is incredibly important. Individually, a few acronyms here and there may not seem so bad, but if a thousand people are making these up, over time the result will be a huge glossary that we have to issue to new employees. [...] This is particularly tough on new employees. [...] The key test for an acronym is to ask whether it helps or hurts communication. An acronym that most engineers outside of SpaceX already know, such as GUI, is fine to use. In practice, most acronyms act as a barrier and not a benefit to clear communication. It makes it harder for new employees to understand what's being discussed. It requires effort for a team to maintain a list of acronym definitions someplace, and overall, it's less of a timesaver to both write and speak than it may seem at first glance."

This may seem blasphemous, or an overbearing and silly rule to try and enforce in a culture. I'm not proposing you punish people for using acronyms or write it on the walls in the halls of your office. Quite the opposite; especially at a smaller organization, it takes only a very light touch to make no-new-acronyms a part of your culture. Get buy-in from your executive team to not create acronyms, and then encourage them to issue a gentle reminder to their managers to do the same, and you'll be amazed how quickly everyone kicks the habit. A sentence or two in your onboarding documentation is often a sufficient nudge for new employees who, due to the gentle note in onboarding and witnessing the lack of acronyms surrounding them, will be far less likely to create them themselves."

## MEETINGS AND TIME MANAGEMENT

Broadly speaking, there are three types of meetings: regularly scheduled informational meetings, conflict resolution meetings, and spontaneous/ ad-hoc meetings. Your job as a manager is to set expectations for attendees based on which type of meeting it is. For informational meetings, ask yourself if a meeting is really the best way to communicate the information; sometimes it is, but not always. If it is, make sure the information is communicated in multiple ways, maybe with written materials provided in advance in your company's wiki. If it's a conflict resolution meeting, make sure you've identified the discussion points in advance so participants can come prepared to discuss and work through the issue. Ad-hoc meetings likely have a clearly defined purpose upfront and need no further introduction.

Regardless of the type of meeting, any meeting you set should have a clear objective that is known to invitees in advance. Ideally, everyone will have enough information before the meeting to know if it'll be valuable for them to attend. Just as importantly, your culture should empower people to make the decision not to attend if they judge it not a good use of their time.

### TIME MANAGEMENT

As a leader at a startup, you'll quickly find your time is split between many kinds of work, and potentially dozens of hours of meetings every week. If you don't yet have a system in place that works for you, now is the time to invest in some good habits and get organized. I recommend both Stephen Covey's *The 7 Habits of Highly Effective People* and David Allen's *Getting Things Done* as places to start on this journey.

### MEETING TIMING

One of the ways you can enable productivity in your team is by creating, or allowing for, large blocks of free time for your engineers. Context switching (our tendency to shift from one unrelated task to another) is expensive (see "The Multitasking Myth" at ctohb.com/myth), so the more time you can create for engineers to do the work of engineering without switching to other tasks (email, phone calls, meetings), the less total context switching penalty you pay.

I'm a fan of declaring an informal "meeting hours" window for the team. Encourage the engineering team, and cross-functional teams, to schedule meetings during this two or three hour window every day and try not to schedule engineers outside that window. That leaves a healthy amount of time *every single day* for your engineering team to focus on the core of their work and also make space for necessary informational and conflict resolution meetings. If your team is in more than three hours of meetings per day (fifteen hours per week, nearly half of their time!), you should take a close look at those meetings and ask yourself if they can be consolidated and reduced.

Other teams have found success with "no-meeting" days—setting aside one or more days each week when nobody schedules any recurring meetings. Just keep in mind that, in a forty-hour work week, your goal is to reserve as many of those hours as possible for your engineering team as contiguous blocks of focus time. A single no-meeting day implies an eight-hour block of focus time, but there are still thirty-two other hours to consider, so it doesn't solve the whole problem.

## ENGINEER'S TIME RECOMMENDATION

Consider this hypothetical week for a software engineer:

- One hour: 1:1 with manager

- Two and a half hours: daily thirty-minute standup meetings

- Two hours: average time spent in other agile ceremonies (sprint planning, retrospectives, etc.)

- Four to eight hours: reviewing others' code

- Four hours: email/chat communication

In total, that's about thirteen to seventeen hours of the week used up for meetings and communication. If you add another few hours on top of that for time spent context switching and unplanned miscellaneous interruptions, quickly you're looking at—at best—half of a forty-hour work week available for actual focus time. If you're not careful about when meetings are scheduled, then not only will your engineers have only twenty hours left for their core tasks, but also they won't have them in contiguous blocks, further reducing productivity.

I present this contrived example to drive home the point that providing engineers with large blocks of focus time to do engineering does not happen by accident. It's up to you as the leader who determines how their time is spent to develop a culture and process that consolidates and minimizes these distractions and maximizes time available for individual contributors to do actual engineering.

## The HIPPO

HIPPO is a casually used industry acronym, short for "Highest-Paid Person's Opinion." Whether you're the highest-paid person or not, your title will imply that you are, and most employees are reluctant to challenge the HIPPO. I strongly encourage you to minimize this effect in discussions by regularly opening the door for challenges, being overtly open to being wrong, and then acting on and championing ideas other than your own. You'll know you're doing this often enough when you feel like you're doing it too often. By the time you feel you're overdoing it, you've probably reached the minimum that most employees need to actually believe you.

In spite of your best efforts to come across as approachable and open to being convinced of other approaches, your presence in a meeting will often still have a subconscious effect on other attendees, especially if they're more than one level below you

> in the organization chart. Be mindful of this effect and do your best to attend meetings only when you truly add value and the team needs you there. For everything else you can get the notes/recording after the meeting is over.

## TO-DO LISTS

In general, to-do lists are a very unsophisticated form of task management, lacking in structure, prioritization, or a time component. I recommend using a calendar-based to-do list. Rather than putting work items in a generic list, slot them in your actual calendar.

This has several advantages. It blocks off dedicated time for actually doing items on your to-do list and ensures you're not overcommitting your time. It allows for prioritization by moving items around, and it also makes it easier to predict when things will get done. Most calendaring systems also have built-in reminder mechanisms that will notify you when you're scheduled to do a particular task.

## CALENDAR RETROSPECTIVES AND TIME BALANCE

Every now and then—say, once a month—I encourage you to do a historic review of your calendar and measure how you've spent your time. For example, Google Calendar has built-in analytics and requires only very minimal adaptation of your calendaring habits to provide accurate summaries of how time was spent. When reviewing this data, ask yourself if the ratio of time spent on various types of activities makes sense for the goals you're trying to achieve. It's also good to check in and confirm that you're spending your time in ways that play to your strengths and bring you personal satisfaction. Often just having this kind of data presented matter-of-factly can provide good motivation for organization and productive change.

## MINI MANAGEMENT FRAMEWORKS

A lot of the problems you'll encounter as a manager follow common, repeating patterns. Having a mental framework to approach problems can speed up decision-making, improve the quality of your decision-making, and provide context and perspective for explaining decisions to others. Below are some frameworks I've found useful in my management journey.

### THREE STAGES OF MANAGEMENT PROBLEM-SOLVING

When presented with a large, ambiguous challenge, such as taking over managing a new team, or diagnosing and improving an individual's under-performance, I like to use a three-step process. These steps should be done sequentially to come up with a plan to address a particular problem.

#### 1. Ingest

Take in as much information as possible. Read available documentation, be it wiki articles, performance reviews, code, or anything you can find related to your problem. Schedule 1:1 meetings, exercise your active listening skills, and take detailed notes on your findings.

You know you've ingested a sufficient amount of data when you start to see the same thing multiple times and you stop seeing new patterns.

Example: multiple people comment about a member of your team's performance, and after a handful of sessions of active listening and getting curious, you've stopped getting further new information on the performance issue.

#### 2. Synthesize

Once you've collected a sufficient body of data related to your problem, take a step back from collecting information and give your brain time to process. I recommend allocating at least a few days at this stage. Try to deliberately stop taking in new information and spend this time looking at the problem from different angles. Take notes, draw diagrams, play golf, take a shower, or whatever helps you think through the problem and come up with an analysis that fits the data and is actionable.

To continue the above example, at this point you might try to come up with various hypotheses for why that individual is underperforming: How are they spending their time? Is it a skills mismatch, an expectations mismatch, or is something going wrong in their personal life, etc.?

## 3. Act

Once you've got a thesis, it's time to actually put a plan into place. When you're taking action, it's important to validate that your plan is achieving the desired results. Whenever possible, test, validate, and—if necessary— start the loop over again.

## TEAM-BASED DECISIONING MODELS

There are three models for developing material for making decisions with your team. As the manager, you can make the material and decisions entirely yourself and present the result as a *fait accompli* to the team. There's also the opposite approach: you start from scratch and entirely codevelop the material with some or all of the team. The third approach is a compromise between the first two: develop a draft yourself and present it as a straw man to the team as a starting point for collecting feedback and iterating to get to a final version. The key differences between these techniques are the amount of time they take, and how much buy-in you get from the team. And I encourage you to optimize for buy-in: ensuring everyone on your team understands decisions and can be a champion for those decisions is the only way to ensure you're all marching in the same direction. As Marty Cagan of Silicon Valley Product Group calls it, you want your team to behave like missionaries, not mercenaries.

- **The Independent Model:** Developing independently as a manager takes the least overall time, but also produces the least buy-in.

- **The Straw Man Model:** Codeveloping decisions starting with a straw man takes a medium amount of time, and—depending on execution—can produce healthy buy-in.

- **The Codevelopment Model:** Developing collectively from scratch can take a significant amount of time, though it produces the most buy-in from those who contributed to the development.

Which model you use for any given decision is up to you, and I encourage you to be thoughtful and deliberate about that choice. Don't be afraid to revisit it if you feel you've chosen the wrong model.

## TWO TYPES OF DECISIONS

In an annual letter to shareholders in 1997, Jeff Bezos outlined a framework for classifying decisions into Type 1 and Type 2 decisions. Type 1 decisions are not reversible, and should be thought through "methodically, carefully, slowly, and with great deliberation and consultation," Bezos wrote. "If you walk through a door and don't like what you see on the other side, you can't get back to where you were before." Which programming language you use, for example, is a Type 1 decision.

Type 2 decisions are the opposite. They "can and should be made quickly by high-judgment individuals or small groups." Which exact shade of gray a button is can be a Type 2 decision, as it's easily changed down the line.

Bezos's advice, which I'll echo here, is that using Type 1 decision-making for Type 2 decisions leads to slowness and failure to experiment and innovate.

Most of your day-to-day technical decisions are Type 2 and are best made quickly and revisited or confirmed after you've collected more data via a prototype or MVP implementation. This is because the most expensive element of most startup technical decisions is the engineering team's time invested in the solution. If you deliberately constrain the time (and thus cost) invested into validating a reversible decision, you're out only a small bit. Most Type 2 technical decisions become irreversible only after you've invested considerable time and new engineering on top of them, so be rigorous about evaluating progress early on. When in doubt, make the decision to reverse early.

## BREAKING TIES

As the leader of your team, ultimately you are accountable for achieving your team's objectives. If the team as a whole fails to meet milestones, that's on you. So, when there is a conflict or disagreement within the team, you need to engage thoughtfully, and then be prepared to make a decision by following one of these three narratives:

- We'll go with your way because you've made a clear and convincing argument that it's superior.

- We'll go with my way because it's superior, and I'll explain why using the additional context I have as a result of being a manager with a broader scope of responsibility.

- We'll go with my way because we can't identify any objective reason why one way is better than another. In other words, it's a tie, and since ultimately I'm the accountable party for success here, we'll go with my approach. I will own the success or failure of this decision.

## Task Triage—The Urgent/Important Matrix

In *The 7 Habits of Highly Effective People*, Dr. Stephen Covey offers the Urgent/Important Matrix, adapted from a concept introduced by President Dwight Eisenhower in a 1955 speech. In the Urgent/Important dichotomy, work is classified by both its urgency (i.e., time sensitivity) and importance (i.e., impact). The result is a four-quadrant chart:

|  | Urgent | Not Urgent |
|---|---|---|
| Important | Crises | Goals & Planning |
| Not Important | Interruptions | Distractions |

I provide this framework here as a reminder to consider the value of various tasks that arise. The tech leader is regularly bombarded by feature requests, debt to prioritize, defects, etc., and having the perspective to ask whether any given item is important and/or urgent is a very useful and quick triage mechanism.

## PEOPLE-PUZZLE SOLVER

Much of the work you'll do as a manager is as a people-puzzle solver. You'll have to figure out how to help two people work together productively, or guide somebody to improve on a skill, or design a team structure to enable collaboration. People's behavior is hard to predict and sometimes a team member may say one thing but think or feel another.

In light of this ever-changing complexity, I encourage you to think like a detective or a scientist: always be collecting data. Form a hypothesis of what might happen if you take a given action, take that action, and then collect data on the results. Going through these motions deliberately will encourage you to listen, to witness how people respond in various scenarios. This in turn will supply helpful data for the next time you're in a similar scenario with the same people.

## JOINING A TEAM

There are two ways you join a team as a technical leader: either you start on a team in a non-leadership position and grow or are promoted into the role, or you're hired to lead a team. If you're promoted into a role, presumably you have good business context and have demonstrated technical competency but have not yet proven yourself in management and leadership. Conversely, if you're being hired into leadership, you likely have a track record in management but lack context, history, and background on the organization's business, technology, and people. It follows, then, that your approach when starting in the role should differ to compensate for the respective weaknesses.

## BEING PROMOTED INTO MANAGEMENT/LEADERSHIP

If you're being promoted into a management role and have invested time in developing management skills, or if you have experience and a track record as a manager, then it's likely you won't find this transition very scary, and your goal will be to continue leveling up as a manager. If this is your first management role, however, you'll have a larger mountain to climb.

People management is an entirely new skill set from the technical skills that got you your promotion. Technical skills are of course a prerequisite to being a good technical manager, but they're far from sufficient. Understanding this, and developing the additional skill set that your new role requires, will be key to succeeding as a manager.

If you were promoted from backend engineer writing code in C to frontend engineer writing code in TypeScript, what kind of things would you do? You might read a book on TypeScript, do some TypeScript coding exercises, join a TypeScript user group, read some TypeScript blogs, etc.

Moving from writing C to managing people is actually a larger change than C to TypeScript. Making this transition successfully requires the same level or more of proactive learning. Becoming a great people manager, for most people, is a lifelong journey, and not a skill picked up in a weekend. Embrace the challenge and treat the job as a lifelong learning exercise that starts now.

## Actionable Management Tips

Keeping in mind German Chancellor Otto von Bismarck's dictum, "Fools learn from experience; I prefer to learn from the experience of others," here are some actionable tips for new managers:

- Find a management mentor or coach. Talking through people's problems and gaining additional perspective is invaluable. (See the sidebar "Find a Management Mentor," page 13.)

- Learn to delegate. *Immunity to Change* by Robert Kegan discusses at length the obstacles to delegation and why learning to delegate is so critical to the success of a manager. The bottom line is that your value to the organization is no longer your own personal output, but that of your team. For many technical leaders, this is the single hardest part of the transition, but it's also the most critical.

- Take care of yourself.
    - Managing people can be very emotionally draining. In order to consistently be your best self, to be level-headed, positive, and productive, it is critical that you take care of yourself.
    - Figure out what works for you; maybe it's meditation, golf, video games, or family time. Do whatever feels good and leaves you refreshed and ready for the next challenge.

○ Pay attention to burnout signs and take a break before it happens. Managing people does not have to be an eighty-hour-a-week activity.

- See the recommended reading list at the end of this book to find more resources for developing your management skills.

## BEING HIRED TO LEAD

If you've been hired to lead a team (as opposed to being promoted into a leadership job or assuming a leadership role as a first-time startup cofounder), presumably you have both technical and management experience. Your challenge as a hired leader of an existing team is to integrate yourself into your new team as smoothly as possible and build trust with your new peers. It should come as no surprise that my advice is to focus more on the people than the technology when managing your new team.

Below, I outline some short-term goals for an externally hired tech leader, plus some questions you should try to answer very early.

Goals:

- Build trust with the technical team. Listen and be thoughtful about when/how quickly you start adding value or changing things.

- Build trust with other teams/leaders, making reasonable commitments and following through on them.

- Learn about the people you're working with and their history with the company/product/technology.

- Diagnose the highest-impact people-specific challenges within the team. Are there staff members who are inappropriately leveled, either underperforming or overperforming their roles? Do any cultural challenges need course correction? Taking decisive action early on to course-correct for culture is a great way to build trust with team members who likely consciously or subconsciously were suffering from the culture issue.

- Diagnose the highest-impact technical problem areas for the team as a whole and put together a set of short-term, medium-term, and long-term objectives for the team.

Questions:

- Who was running technology before? Is that person still on the team? It's common for tech leaders to discover that they want to grow into people management. Where this has happened, you'll be stepping into a people management void. The other common scenario is that either there was no prior tech leader or they've left the job due to underperformance, and you are inheriting a large amount of tech debt.

- What problem does the CEO say you were hired to solve?

- What problem do you think you were hired to solve?

- What pain points exist between the technical team and the rest of the company today?

- What pain points are the highest priority within the technical team?

## Giving Technical Advice to Friends/Strangers

After you've had some form of technical leadership on your résumé for a while, you'll likely start to get friends, or friends of friends, reaching out for advice. For the most part, I recommend taking these phone calls, not only because the networking is valuable, but because the questions you are asked may force you to think through and put words to ideas you're subconsciously working on. They say teaching others is the best way to really learn something yourself.

A quick note on advising non-technical founders: you're likely to get approached from time to time by somebody with a self-pro-claimed billion-dollar idea. It costs very little to take these calls and can be a great way to build some social/relationship capital. Be mindful however that brilliant ideas don't themselves make successful businesses. Between every great idea and success is a gigantic mountain of execution, and most climbers aren't equipped to summit Everest. So be very careful about making commitments to someone with a good idea and no climbing gear.

## TRAFFIC: FUNNELS AND UMBRELLAS

"You can either be a shit funnel or a shit umbrella."
Todd Jackson, Gmail Product Manager
(see ctohb.com/umbrella and ctohb.com/keytogmail.)

Questions, concerns, and ideas about your product, absent any strict process for directing them elsewhere, will find their way to management. That includes not just you but everyone in management in your organization. Managers are the default inbox, and the crux of Jackson's statement is that your team is the default outbox. You hear, "Hey, there's a bug in X," and you think, "OK, engineer Y wrote that feature, go send them the bug." That would be an example of funneling inbound directly at your team.

A better strategy is instead to act as an umbrella for the team. Rather than directing all the inbound in real time to the team, a good manager organizes, prioritizes, and gives the team a structured queue to work with. Your goal is to help the team focus, limit distraction, and provide a place for where inbound should go so it can be efficiently processed.

Only on rare occasions should you, as manager, highlight a bug to an individual engineer. If you have a bug queue and a process for working through that queue, you can largely eliminate regular one-off escalations.

Management should be monitoring that bug queue process to ensure the queue stays at a manageable length, and adjusting staffing or process if product quality isn't meeting targets.

You should prioritize your queues based on importance and urgency. If something of critical importance with extreme time pressure arises, it should be put into the queue and escalated to the top. Then apply common sense as to how you handle it. If you need to call somebody to ensure they know it's there, then so be it, as long as this is the exception and not the rule.

## YOUR FIRST TEAM

As a technical leader, your job is not just to manage the technical team; it also includes serving as the technical representative in the C-suite. Your role is to represent engineering and technology in all of the company's highest-level strategic discussions and to ensure that engineering and technology are on the right course for the business. At times, this means having difficult conversations with other leaders—conversations that require vulnerability and humility, and conversations that enable you to work through conflict and are grounded in mutual trust. These conversations are key to the job, and for them to be possible you must be deeply engaged with your leadership team, thinking of them as your "first" team.

You're likely a highly technical person. You probably enjoy your technical meetings the most, or at least find solving technical problems with your team familiar and highly satisfying. So, it's easy to fall into a pattern where you spend most of your time with technical teams, and to adopt a "my team is the technical team" mindset. This is a great way to build rapport within the tech team, and there are times when that is the most critical relationship to invest in.

My guidance is simple: do not let the technical shiny objects distract you or limit your investment in relationships with non-technical leaders. Your relationships with other leaders and your trust with your non-technical peers will give you credibility and enable you to guide the business to making good technical decisions as a whole. Building trust outside the technical team is built the same way any other trust relationship is built: great communication, regular expectation setting by making and meeting commitments, and owning up to mistakes/failures if and when they occur.

The technical leader or CTO who spends all their time deep in code with engineering and barely participates in the leadership team will have little credibility when trying to convince the other C-levels to invest further in engineering. Or worse, they won't even be asked for their input when the time comes to make a hard call. Other leaders will not have the context to understand the value of what the tech team is asking for or the perspective on how engineering is operating at that moment, and they'll lack the shared vision for what it can be in the future. Only by regularly engaging with the rest of the leadership team, sharing that context, and being part of the conversation along the way can you, as the technical leader, ensure that the leadership team has a shared understanding of how engineering helps the organization and how it needs to grow over time.

## WORKING WITH THE CEO

Every CTO–CEO relationship is different, though there are a few elements that are common to all such partnerships, as well as some key prerequisites for a healthy relationship.

### ALIGNING SPECIFIC OBJECTIVES

The CEO must have complete trust in your ability to lead the technical team to meet business objectives. Building that trust means you need to be able to communicate well with the CEO, both through proactive communication and making sure the CEO always has enough context to ask good questions.

Communicating well means learning to speak business language and avoiding lapses into tech jargon during leadership conversations. You want to empower the CEO to communicate with you, and the more you speak their language (if they aren't technical), the more information you can get out of your interactions, and the better the two of you will get along.

### ALIGNING BUSINESS DIRECTION

You and the CEO need to have a shared understanding of the direction of the business and be able to engage in constructive—and perhaps even contentious—conversations to ensure the depth of that understanding. Trust applies to overall business direction as well as specific objectives. There are many ways to build this, but you need to establish trust regardless of the approach you take. Engage in shared non-work activities, find areas where you share personal values, and use specific tools and exercises to build that trust (see Brené Brown's BRAVING Inventory at ctohb. com/braving).

## ALIGNING CULTURE AND VALUES

As with all C-levels, the CTO and CEO should have strong alignment on company culture and values. It's particularly important that you focus on building a positive culture within engineering, and between engineering and the rest of the company. The technical team is often a very large—if not the single largest—line item in a startup company's budget. Technical staff are also often the most competitive roles to hire for, making recruiting—and inevitable involuntary employee turnover—more expensive in engineering than in other departments.

Strong alignment between the CTO and other C-level executives on culture and values is a key factor in ensuring the technical team feels respected and included in the company, which should in turn help with retention.

## DELIVERING BAD NEWS

One general piece of advice for working with other leaders or executives is to not shy away from delivering bad news to your fellow leaders, especially the CEO. Since you are accountable for the performance of the team, you may be tempted to sugarcoat reality, to advertise that everything is fine. The problems with this approach are numerous:

- If things are not fine, meaning deadlines are consistently missed or quality is falling below expectations, your peers will know that and will wonder why you're not owning those failures and explaining how you'll improve. This disparity between reality and how you're representing it undermines trust in your leadership.

- From time to time, you'll need to make time for the software engineering team to do non-user-facing engineering as an investment, either in tech debt or future architecture. You'll need to have the trust of other leaders and the credibility so that others believe you and understand the ROI on that time.

See the "Principle" section of Chapter 1 of Jocko Willink and Leif Babin's *Extreme Ownership: How U.S. Navy SEALs Lead and Win* for more on the importance of owning failure.

## SPEAKING THE LANGUAGE OF YOUR AUDIENCE

Technical topics are often highly nuanced; the details matter. Technical jargon does a great job at helping to convey that nuance, so it's no surprise that when engineers explain technical subjects they often use language that is unintelligible to members of other departments. I'm sure you've witnessed the over-eager engineer trying, with energy, passion, and excitement, to explain their project to a non-engineer only to be met with a blank stare and no new shared understanding being created. As a technical leader, you must do better.

If, for example, you have a major area of tech debt and you want to advocate within the executive team for taking an entire month to re-architect that area of code, you need to communicate your reasons in a comprehensible way. If you enter that conversation discussing latencies, RPC calls, dependency injection, and acronyms from your cloud service provider, chances are your CEO and CFO will tune you out almost immediately.

If, on the other hand, you frame that conversation around developer productivity and team morale, and explain the debt paydown in the context of team velocity over the next six months, your argument will be much more convincing.

### Technical Communication Best Practices

A few general tips for ensuring more successful discussions and presentations—particularly with non-engineers—when talking tech:

- Establish a shared language/vocabulary upfront. If you need to use any words the average high-school student wouldn't understand, make sure that your audience already knows them, or clearly define them before launching into the explanation.

- Use relatable concepts. Technical challenges are often compared to other technical challenges: that does not work when talking to non-technical staff. Rather than describing your slow data transfer in bytes per second, compare it to traffic on a highway.
- Confirm understanding along the way. Ask questions of your audience during your explanation. If they can say the punchline before you then you know you're on the right track.
- Don't assume you are in any way superior due to your mastery of technical language, or worse, make your audience feel inferior for their lack of knowledge. "I don't want to get too technical for you" is a great way to turn off an audience.
- In general, try to keep your explanations as simple and concise as you can. Avoid going down rabbit holes that might be a distraction or otherwise disengage your audience.

# 1.2 Hiring and Interviewing

Hiring effectively is one of your highest-impact activities as a technical leader—and one of the most challenging to get right. You will often find yourself trying to recruit talent in a supply-constrained market and competing against other companies that might have deeper pockets than yours. Your top candidates will likely receive other competing job offers, which means you not only need to qualify candidates but convince them that your opportunity is the right one for them.

In that way, hiring is as much a sales activity (where candidates qualify you/your company) as it is a filtering process (you/your company qualifies the candidates). It's important to keep this in mind every step of the way as you define your team's hiring processes.

This section of the book covers the various sections of the hiring and interviewing journey, sequentially, from headcount planning to onboarding.

## HIRE LIKE A STARTUP

As a startup, you have several key advantages in hiring, and it's critical you leverage those in the process to ensure you can attract top talent. A few features that give you an edge:

- You're smaller, meaning you should also be more nimble, higher-touch, and faster to hire than "large" competition.

- You can sell a highly compelling company and personal growth trajectory.

- You can sell a creative and inspiring workplace culture.

- You can sell the impact that successful candidates will make.

- You can offer meaningful equity ownership in the company and thus the ability to share in the upside of the company's success.

Here are some practical tips for leveraging these advantages:

- To move fast, train and enlist coworkers for interviews before posting the job description. Make sure that everyone understands the scheduling process, the interview scripts, and scoring criteria, and how to use the Applicant Tracking Software (ATS) to read and leave feedback before you even get started (see Sourcing Candidates, page 59).

- Schedule all the interviews with each candidate upfront. If your process includes four interviews, get all four on the calendar at the start, ideally within five business days. If your team is quick about leaving their interview feedback (and you should insist that they are), then you can give any candidates that fail out early notice and cancel any pending calendar invitations. The alternative—scheduling subsequent interviews only after a candidate passes each round—adds multiple days in between each step, easily turning what could be a week-long process into three weeks or more.

- A good rule of thumb, especially at a startup: nobody is too busy or too important to make themselves available to meet with candidates if it makes sense for them to do so, especially for more senior hires. If a strong candidate asks to talk to your CEO and COO, then you should schedule meetings with them.

- Ensure that each interviewer has a unique script or guide that covers different material, or material from a different angle than other interviews. (For more detail on this, see the "Ask Only New Questions" section of Interviewing Best Practices, page 63.)

As ever, there is no free lunch, and the benefits of hiring as a startup also come with tradeoffs, primarily in the form of risk. Candidates are almost certain to ask you questions about your company's product market fit, cash on hand or runway, company culture, and work/life balance. I encourage you to be candid with candidates about these factors, work with your executive team on the facts on the ground, and have good answers to these questions when asked.

## Speed is Your Friend

Remember, speed is your friend when recruiting top talent. If you can move somebody through your full process in a week, you give your startup a major advantage against larger companies whose processes often take months to arrive at a decision.

## WHEN TO HIRE: HEADCOUNT PLANNING

Cash is the lifeblood of a young and not-yet-profitable startup, so the decision to commit to a recurring $100,000-plus a year expense in the form of a new engineer's salary should not be taken lightly. Several key factors contribute to headcount decisions, foremost among them need, prioritization, timing, and budget.

### ROLE NEED/TEAM GAP

The first step toward deciding to hire is identifying a gap in the team. Gaps come in several forms. Commonly, at an early stage in a company's development, it's simply a skill gap. For example, your business decides that mobile apps are going to be a key element of your go-to-market strategy, and your founding team has never worked in mobile before. Certainly, they could learn and become effective over time, but it would be far more efficient in both the short and long term to hire a senior engineer who has experience in and desire to work on mobile to build and maintain that project.

Other kinds of gaps include seniority gaps (not enough senior experience to make good decisions, or not enough junior talent to handle less complex tasks), management gaps (one manager responsible for too many people), or subject matter expertise gaps (no one on the team who understands an area of the industry well enough to guide decision-making).

The other major justification for a hire is to increase total bandwidth on a team. These kinds of hires should be aligned with some kind of business objective, or product roadmap, that justifies bringing on a new permanent team member at a given time.

## ROLE PRIORITIZATION AND TIMING

Once you've identified a gap, the next question to ask is when that gap needs to be filled. Taking into account the lead time required to get a great hire, when does it make sense to start the hiring process?

Often—though not always—the answer is "right now!" Every new person you hire adds complexity and overhead to your team. Assuming the pain of having the gap isn't severe, if you can get away with a smaller team for another six months and delay the hire, that can be a good idea as it both reduces cost and gives you more time to build a case for the hire.

Headcount or hiring requests from your team will often have to compete with requests from other teams, so it's useful to develop a common language across your company for discussing how urgent or important a hire is. This doesn't have to be very sophisticated; it could be a 0–5 ranking system, where a 0 represents an urgent need, and a 5 a hire that would be nice to have but can wait a few months or quarters before becoming urgent.

## BUDGETING FOR NEW HIRES

At an unprofitable startup, you should have a financial model that rationalizes expenses vs. revenue and forecasts roughly how long your current cash on hand will last before you need another fundraising round. Most

CEOs and CFOs have a deep and intimate understanding of this model; as a tech leader, you won't need to spend nearly as much time with it.

However, it's essential that you maintain a clear picture of your department's contribution to that model, which will primarily come in the form of headcount expenses (current and future). This model should provide some level of constraint, in the form of either an annualized budget or an expense run-rate, that will guide the timing of your hires.

## HIRING GOALS AND OBJECTIVES

Just as with designing software systems, when you sit down to design your interview process, you should begin by considering your requirements and goals. While every company should and will have its own requirements and perspective, here are some of the things I consider when designing an interview process:

- **Efficiency:** How much time and cost does it take to hire a candidate?

- **Success rate:** How successful on the job are hired candidates and how long do they stay with the firm?

- **Candidate experience:** Do candidates come away thinking highly of your company after going through the process, regardless of whether they were hired?

- **Equitable opportunities:** Have you ensured that every person has a fair shot at being hired, and avoided unconscious bias as much as possible?

- **Scalability:** Can people other than you run the process and be as effective/have a success rate similar to yours?

## EFFICIENCY

Hiring well is an expensive undertaking for your company. That cost comes in actual dollars, be it for recruiters, job board listings, or job advertisements. It also costs time, primarily in employee time spent conducting interviews. As you design your interview process, consider what your intention is with each step, what you are filtering for, and what is the most efficient way to accomplish that filtering.

One way to reduce—or at least spread out—the time investment is to include other team members in the hiring process. Depending on the subject matter of a given interview, you don't always need your most senior engineers in the room. A hiring coordinator, with appropriate training, can do a phone screen, a culture interview, or a reference check just as effectively as a senior engineer or executive.

## SUCCESS RATE

Not every hire is going to be a home run for your company. Some will be leveled incorrectly, some won't be a culture fit, and others will be fired or quit in the first year. Especially as you scale an interview process, you need to measure how many hires are successful. This is one of the few opportunities as a technical leader where you can calculate clear, consistent, and indicative metrics, so take advantage and ensure your process is top notch. Consider tracking time to hire (from posting a job description until a new hire start date), overall employee retention, new hire attrition (or down-leveling), as well as how many new hires are promoted in their first two years.

As Andy Grove discusses in *High Output Management*, even a world-class interview process is successful only about 70 percent of the time. Fundamentally, there are many risks in hiring: you're trying to predict how someone will perform forty hours a week, week in and week out, based on just a few conversations and data points gathered in an interview process. The best leaders track their success rate, aren't afraid of admitting hiring mistakes, and will "hire slow, fire fast."

There's no getting around it: firing a new employee who isn't working out shortly after they were hired is socially awkward and uncomfortable for everyone. It is, however, the responsible thing to do for your team. Some practices to help provide transparency to new employees and assist managers in making good decisions include implementing a formal ninety-day "probationary" or "introductory" period and required new-employee/manager check-ins every fifteen or thirty days, or using a contract-to-hire employment structure.

## CANDIDATE EXPERIENCE

Candidate experience is how candidates feel about your company during and after they go through your hiring process. Many candidates will do due diligence on your company before applying or interviewing. They're likely to look at online forums and social media and see what other candidates or employees who went through your process have to say about you.

You can't always control what people say about you, but nonetheless, you want to provide the sort of candidate experience that makes them more likely to read good things online, have a great experience themselves, and thus be more inclined to continue with your interviews and accept your offers.

## EQUITABLE OPPORTUNITIES

There's a saying that "people tend to hire people who look like themselves." This is often the result of unsophisticated interview scoring methods that simply rely on an interviewer's gut feeling, and gut feelings are often strongly influenced by unconscious bias. This bias can disadvantage candidates of other races, genders, ethnicities, etc.

As you design your interview process, you should focus on evaluations based on a rubric that aligns with requirements from a job description, not just an interviewer's gut feeling. See the "Avoiding Bias" section in Interviewing Best Practices, page 63, for more about avoiding biases.

## SCALABILITY

It's all well and good if you, individually, are capable of hiring effectively. At some point, there will be more open roles than you can hire yourself, and you'll need to scale the process and bring in other people. To do so effectively, you must build a repeatable system that others can leverage to identify top talent and hire with the same efficacy and success rate as you. That means that somebody else will need to be able to conduct the same interviews and draw the same conclusions at the end of that process that you likely would have if you'd conducted the interviews yourself.

The goal of the remainder of this section is to help you create a scalable system for interviewing and hiring that fits your organization's goals and can work seamlessly *without* your direct involvement (once you've taken the time to calibrate it). By defining and deploying this kind of structure, creating thoughtful documentation, and templating, you enable others to conduct interviews and produce candidate ranking scores that would closely mirror your own.

## THE JOB DESCRIPTION

Many companies underestimate the value of a great job description. A really good job description does two main things for you: it helps you create clarity and alignment internally with your company on what the role does and the value it can offer, and it advertises your company and attracts the kind of applicants that could be a good fit.

### Surveying the Market

Before starting to write a job description I encourage you to do a survey of the market. Look at competing or similar companies and the job descriptions they have for similar roles.

Often these posts can provide good inspiration and calibration, especially when you're hiring for less common roles that may not be as well addressed by the scalable system you've put in place.

## CREATING CLARITY ON A ROLE

The traditional job description has a brief description of what the role will do, followed by a bulleted list of requirements for the candidate. I encourage you to write more than that. Rather than focusing on what a successful candidate will do in a particular role, think through the purpose the role serves. What outcomes does the role drive? What kind of impact do you expect from this role in three, six, or twelve months? You may or may not want to publish the answer to these questions as part of the job description, but the exercise of going into detail on expectations will prove valuable nonetheless.

Socialize the answers to these questions with other leaders at your organization and ensure they agree with the answers. Don't be surprised if you get significant feedback on the first version of the responsibilities and outcomes of a role. At most startups, before a headcount is formally opened, there is a high-level, unstructured conversation around a specific title. "Oh, we need to hire a senior JavaScript backend engineer." The act of writing and socializing the job description enables your team to get precise about what the company really needs, so it's natural that you'll need to do a few revisions.

## JOB DESCRIPTIONS AS AN ADVERTISEMENT

Everything your company posts publicly is a reflection of your culture and brand. A job description is no exception. The job description targets the single most valuable customer of that culture and brand: your employees, present and future. Ideally, the right candidate—someone who not only meets your job requirements but who is also a great culture fit—reads your job description and is excited about both the role and the company itself.

Some ways to help your job description reflect your culture:

- Include your company's core values, mission, or vision—whatever you have—front and center.

- Include the impact that the role will have on your team, company, and customers.

- Advertise your team structure, working environment, and size.

- Highlight your compensation and benefits (posting a salary range is legally required in some markets).

In addition to elements aimed to pique candidate interest, it's a good idea to include some often-overlooked details to help candidates self-tier:

- Include leveling and compensation brackets.

- Include location, on-site requirements, and whether remote work is allowed and to what extent.

- Include time zone/working hour requirements.

## SOURCING CANDIDATES

When it comes to filling roles in your organization, you'll source qualified candidates in three ways: inbound recruiting, outbound recruiting, and referrals. An effective, scalable hiring process should be designed to leverage all three methods.

### INBOUND RECRUITING

Inbound recruiting is about marketing your job opening and collecting voluntary candidate applications. Much like any other marketing exercise, a one-channel approach may not be enough to drive results. As such, posting a job description on a job board is the bare minimum. Depending on the state of the market, how many roles you're hiring for, and the quality/clarity of your job description, the posting alone may be sufficient. Often you'll need to do more to draw in top talent, including actively promoting your roles in specialized tech communities and/or marketing your brand via conference attendance/sponsorship, a company blog, social media outreach, etc.

There is no universal best venue for placing classified ads that great employees turn to. Keep your ear to the ground for whatever platform/job site seems to be most common and post your job description accordingly. This is something a good Applicant Tracking System (ATS) will help you with, as it can track a referral source for every candidate and provide metrics around which job boards bring in better/more candidates that make it deeper into your process than others. When hiring designers in particular, it's important to talk to some working designers about where the most popular portfolio hosting sites are and maintain a presence on those job boards to find the best candidates.

You'll also want to monitor how many applications you're receiving for each role. At a minimum, your hiring manager(s) should be looking at the state of the funnel for their roles on a weekly basis and adjusting their approach accordingly. If a role isn't getting enough applicants (or is attracting the wrong applicants), then change something! Try tweaking the job title or posting the job description to new channels. A key element of a strong hiring process is the same as any other process you build for your team: a humble willingness to revisit past decisions and improve over time.

## OUTBOUND RECRUITING

Outbound recruiting involves proactively reaching out to target candidates and encouraging them to apply for your role. This can be done by you, your team, an internal recruiter, and/or an external recruiter. I encourage teams to start their hiring process with inbound recruiting and in-house outbound recruiting first. By actually doing the recruiting, talking to the candidates, and listening to their reactions to your pitch, you'll learn a lot about the market and what top candidates think of what you're selling. You'll also get a sense of how competitive your offer is and how easy or hard it is to find candidates that match your job description, perhaps even leading you to tweak it. Once you've fine-tuned the role and know exactly whom and what you're looking for, you'll be ready to give optimized guidance to an external recruiter, which will help them source candidates more effectively on your behalf.

Not all external recruiters are the same. You want somebody who meets all of these criteria:

- Highly organized

- Able to effectively sell your role (it's your job to train and hold them accountable to do this well)

- Motivated to follow up relentlessly without being pushy or obnoxious

- Inclined to value the relationship with both you and the candidate more than the commission for a single placement

## REFERRALS

The highest return on investment in hiring comes from internal referrals, i.e., referrals from your existing employees. People are much more likely to want to do business with a company that is spoken highly of by a current team member, and it's often easier to find a cultural fit when the candidate has already been vetted by someone familiar with your culture. You can encourage internal referrals by providing cash incentives (see sidebar) or having good communication with referees as to the status of their referrals.

Given that referrals have such a high chance of success, you want to provide the best possible candidate experience. You may also want to consider an abbreviated (but fair) hiring process. Skipping or compressing any top-of-funnel coarse filters, such as phone screeners or qualification forms, may be appropriate. You may also want to encourage the referrer to contribute a paragraph or two, in writing, justifying their referral.

### A Note on the Mathematics of Incentivizing Referrals

Based on the data you likely already have, it's relatively easy to approximate the cost (in both time and actual dollars spent) to hire a new engineer for your company. If you consider that referrals often have a substantially higher conversion rate to hire, it becomes clear that referrals save thousands to tens of thousands of dollars, which can help you justify a multi-thousand-dollar bonus to any employee who refers a candidate who is ultimately hired and stays in their role for more than a few months.

## INTERVIEWING BEST PRACTICES

The interview flow is where the rubber meets the road on your ability to determine how well a candidate fits the role you're hiring for. Keep in mind that there is no perfect interview. The amount of data an interviewer collects in a sparse few hours with a candidate, of course, cannot perfectly predict how well somebody will do full-time on the job for months and years to come.

In this section, I cover some high-level interviewing best practices, and then provide some background and context on the various steps of interviewing, including candidate/résumé intake forms, phone screens, culture interviews, technical interviews, coding assignments, or take-home assignments, executive interviews, and—finally—reference checks.

### REJECTED CANDIDATES' OPINIONS MATTER

When designing your interview process, your candidate experience should be top of mind and a top priority. Even if you choose not to hire a candidate, that person will walk away with an impression—good or bad—of you and your company. That impression may lead to them singing your praises to those in their professional network who may someday apply for your roles. Or that impression could lead them to rant negatively about you every chance they get.

Job boards and Google reviews are littered with the evidence of interviews running amok, and it's very difficult to undo the damage to your reputation once it's been done. While it's true that, for some candidates, no amount of respect and consideration on your part will prevent the bitter sting of rejection from poisoning their takeaway opinion of you, those people are in the minority. For most candidates who get to the interview stage, a respectful and thoughtful interviewing process will leave them with a neutral-to-positive feeling about your company and help you avoid negative press online.

## BE TIMELY AND MAKE SCHEDULING EASY

Ideally, you/your team will communicate the steps and scope of your hiring process to candidates upfront and leverage an easy, reliable solution for scheduling those steps in real time. For example, you can choose to (A) designate a hiring manager to handle all of the scheduling during business hours, (B) schedule all of the interviews in advance, or (C) provide an online tool that candidates can use to schedule their interviews asynchronously on their own time.

Truly, anything is better than requiring each interviewer to email each candidate before each interview to set up schedules sequentially, which can drag out an interview process over weeks or months.

## ASK ONLY NEW QUESTIONS

Every interview touchpoint should feel to the candidate like a continuation of the conversation, rather than a rehashing of details that were discussed in prior sessions. Avoiding the latter requires thoughtful structuring and careful planning in advance of your interviews.

Ideally, subsequent interviews should be used to dive deeper and explore areas specific to a candidate or role, where both parties are looking to fully understand key strengths and weaknesses. Sharing suggested areas to focus on or new questions to ask with subsequent interviewers via an Applicant Tracking System (ATS) is a great way to ensure continuity, efficiency, and a great candidate experience that can reveal whether or not your potential hires are a true fit for your team.

## AVOID BIASES

If you're unfamiliar with the phrase "unconscious bias," I encourage you to read *Thinking Fast and Slow* by Daniel Kahneman. It's my go-to book for understanding many types of systematic errors our brains make.

It's actually very easy to unintentionally advantage or disadvantage a candidate in ways that are not justified. Inevitably, this will result in worse hiring outcomes—or potentially costly legal battles.

Bias takes many forms. Most biases are unconscious and can surround gender, race, alumni status, or socioeconomic background. But bias can also mean that the conclusions drawn by an interviewer about a candidate ahead of an interview are based solely on ranking scores from a prior interviewer. There's no system that ensures eliminating all harmful biases, but there are certain steps you can take to minimize unconscious bias, such as blanking out candidate names or photos (which often hint at gender and ethnicity) during a résumé screen.

To avoid anchoring or biasing subsequent interviewers, I encourage interviewers to leave two different kinds of feedback on candidate conversations:

1. Detailed notes and scores

2. Suggested questions for subsequent conversations.

Most of the interview feedback should consist of detailed notes and scores against the job-specific scoring guide which has your interview questions planned out in advance (for more, see Technical Interviews, page 76). This feedback should ideally not be read by subsequent team members in advance of their interview to avoid bias. For example, if you know the prior interviewer scored the candidate poorly, you may experience confirmation bias and overvalue any areas where a candidate does poorly in your interview.

The second type of feedback, subsequent interview suggestions, should focus on areas for emphasis or more in-depth exploration in subsequent interviews and not reveal data that might overtly bias further interviews.

## USAGE OF AN APPLICANT TRACKING SYSTEM (ATS)

When interviewing more than two or three candidates simultaneously, it can require a substantial effort to manage the logistics of where candidates stand in the process, coordinate notes from interviewers, and communicate consistently and promptly with candidates as they move through the funnel. Without a finely tuned system to manage all of these logistics, it's easy for candidate experience to suffer and for hiring costs to rise. This is a universal problem, and several high-quality, off-the-shelf Applicant Tracking System (ATS) solutions have been developed at various price points and levels of sophistication to address this problem.

The guidance here is simple: choose and onboard an ATS early. Don't wait until your process is already underwater to take action. Train your team, require widespread adoption of the system, and set expectations for its use with HR, hiring managers, and interviewers.

## SELLING CANDIDATES

As mentioned earlier, I highly encourage hiring managers to think of the interview process as a sales process. This naturally leads to several good habits that translate seamlessly from sales to interviews:

- During the sales process with a customer, you're always focused on selling the prospect on the product, even when you're qualifying the customer. A good sales process regards qualifying candidates as a funnel, with light-touch qualification at the top and progressively more nuanced/time-intensive qualification down-funnel, along with a progressively more customized and tailored sales pitch.

- You should always be selling your candidates on the advantages and positive benefits of joining your company and the role/opportunity you're offering. By the time they jump through all your interviewing hoops, they should be eager to work at your company and excited to take your job offer over others they have received (or may yet receive).

- Ensure you're asking at least a couple of open-ended questions early on about what the candidate is looking for in their next role. This will help your interviewers synthesize how good a match the candidate's expectations are for the role you're hiring for. This information should be noted in the candidate's profile and used to tailor and customize the pitch to the candidate along the way.
  - For example, a junior candidate coming from a mostly junior and mid-level team may be looking for the opportunity to work

with more senior JavaScript engineers in an environment that promotes their growth. If your team offers senior support and your culture leans into mentorship, make sure you highlight that advantage, especially around the offer stage.

- Always leave candidates some time (five or ten minutes) to ask questions at the end of the interview. Most qualified candidates come to interviews armed with questions, and you can learn a lot about what somebody cares about by what they choose to ask. This is a good opportunity for your interviewer to sell the benefits of your company in their responses.

- Along the way, ensure candidates feel respected and are progressively exposed to more of your company. Your best candidates need to feel like they were intelligently vetted *and* like they've learned enough about the company to get excited. Ideally, you want even rejected candidates to be able to leave positive reviews on Google and Glassdoor. You can accomplish that by selling your company's benefits throughout the interview, respecting people's time as if it were your own, having consistent and timely communication, and ensuring that everyone feels the process was as fair and transparent as possible.

## INTAKE FORMS

The beginning of the interview funnel is a form that achieves two goals: it provides the candidate with some information about your company and its hiring process, and thus a sample of its culture; and it takes in a bunch of information from the candidate to act as an inexpensive, coarse-grained filter.

### Intake Form Preamble

At the top of your intake form, you should outline several key pieces of information for candidates:

- Reiterate the role they are applying for and its key requirements and impact.

- Reiterate your company's core values and provide a sample of your culture.

- Set expectations for the hiring process, how long it will take, how many steps there are, and generally what the process looks like.

### Intake Form Questionnaire

The questionnaire should include a request for the candidate's résumé (or LinkedIn profile URL), ask some questions required by legal and HR with respect to employment eligibility, and then ideally ask a few qualifying questions of the candidate. The qualifying questions should be light-touch, generally freeform, and possibly even technical questions to ensure the candidate is in the right ballpark for the role. For example, for a role that requires experience in JavaScript, it's not unreasonable to confirm that experience in the questionnaire with a question like, "Rate your comfort level working with JavaScript on a scale from 'not comfortable' to 'extremely comfortable.'"

This may seem redundant to the requirements listed in the job description, and it is, though you'd be surprised how many résumés will come through lacking basic qualifications. These questions are quick/trivial for the candidate to answer and just as quick for a hiring manager to use to filter out applicants.

If you're inundated with candidates and want to do a bit more filtering at this stage, the questionnaire can also include one or two more interesting or difficult questions. If you include these, be sure to still keep them brief; you don't want to lose candidates in this form because the questions were too arduous. If you're overwhelmed with applicants then bias towards more data to filter with here, otherwise maybe it's best to save more nuanced qualifications for further down the funnel.

Some example questions for an intake form covering broad compatibility and self-identified technical familiarity (I've included a sample at ctohb. com/templates):

- As a great candidate, you'll receive a ton of offers. Compensation and benefits being equal, what will make you pick one company over another?

- What are deal makers and deal breakers in your next move?

- What gives you energy in your work? What taxes your energy?

- What are your geographic expectations (location, remote, on-site)?

- How familiar are you with basic technical qualifiers: rank familiarity with [relevant programming language or tool] on a scale of 1–10?

## PHONE SCREEN

The initial phone screen, like everything in the interview process, serves a dual function: it's an opportunity to learn more about the candidate, and it's the candidate's first interaction with (and evaluation of) a human at your company.

Given that this is the first person the candidate will have an interaction with at your company, it's worth thinking carefully about who conducts the interview. The questions at this point should not be very technical in nature and so it's not necessary that the interview be conducted by a member of the technical team. Often it is done by HR or a dedicated recruiting team.

Regardless of who runs the phone screen, ensure that person is a good cultural representative for your team/company and is equipped with the information technical candidates are likely to ask for at this stage, including:

- What the software stack looks like, including key languages, tools, and target clients (e.g., mobile, desktop, etc.). The interviewer should have a rudimentary understanding of the words they are using here, and not just reading off a list.

- The size of the technical team, both at large in the company and that the candidate would be working with. This should also include general hiring forecasts and roughly how many people are being added over time.

- Who the candidate would be reporting to. Provide some basic background on that manager, including their tenure at the company, maybe what they did before working at the company.

- A great sense of the company's core values/culture and way of doing work.

The interviewer's goal should be to introduce the candidate to the company, its culture, the role, and the hiring process. They will also ask some high-level questions of the candidate to confirm their structural fit for the role. You want a candidate to walk away from this interview motivated to do well in the rest of the interview process and excited at the idea of working for your company.

The exact questions asked in a phone screen are thus not super important. Here is an outline of some areas you may want to cover:

- Do they have anything constraining their hiring timeline (e.g., other job offers)?

- Where is the candidate located, and are they willing to relocate if necessary?

- Roughly when can they start or are they looking to start?

- Confirm compensation expectations are aligned and explain benefits/perks.

In addition to good answers to the questions, the interviewer should gauge their general fit for the role. Does the candidate communicate clearly, do they seem like a culture fit, does their claimed experience match what they have on their résumé, and are they interested in the company and opportunity?

## CULTURE INTERVIEW

One of the major criteria you're looking for in your interview process is culture fit. Culture fit is all the elements of a candidate's personality, beyond their experience and skills, that will enable them to be successful in your organization. In order to effectively screen candidates for culture fit, your company should have a fairly clear idea of what its culture is. This can look like many things--for example, a list of core values, a mission statement, a vision statement, guiding principles. Whatever they are, they should be authentic and true to the company. If you're struggling on this, I would refer you to *Team of Teams* by Stanley McChrystal, *Work Rules!* by Laszlo Bock, and *Good Authority* by Jonathan Raymond.

Currently, there are few formally structured interview programs that are widely used. The one that does come up fairly regularly is called "topgrading," which refers to at least two different things: the topgrading method and the topgrading interview. The topgrading method (ctohb.com/topgrading) is an entire book hiring methodology that was purportedly developed by General Electric in the 1980s/90s and written about in Verne Harnish's *Scaling Up*. The topgrading interview (ctohb.com/interview), which I call the culture interview, is a specific interview agenda, style, and structure designed to learn about a candidate's background and cultural fit.

As formally designed, the topgrading interview walks a candidate through their employment history and asks the same set of questions about each of the candidate's prior few roles. Depending on the candidate's history and how long they spent at their past few roles, you should cover anywhere from two to five past positions. You want to capture a long enough period of time to try and identify trends and see growth, but also not keep the candidate in the interview for three hours discussing internships they had in college twenty years ago.

For each role, topgrading has the interviewer ask the following questions:

- What were some notable successes or accomplishments in this position?

- What were some mistakes or failures in this position?

- What was your supervisor's name and title?

- What do you think the supervisor's honest assessment of your strengths and weaknesses would be?

- What do you feel your supervisor's strengths and weaknesses were?

In addition to this interview formula, topgrading suggests a two-interviewer approach: the lead, who is actively engaging in conversation and getting curious with the candidate; and a dedicated notetaker.

Whether you're using one or two interviewers, taking notes is critically important. To review candidates fairly, you will want to create a scorecard in advance of interviewing your first candidate which evaluates a candidate's answers, looking for alignment to your company culture. For example, if respectful challenge is a company core value, ask the candidate if they could identify any instances of challenging respectfully. Or did they speak disrespectfully about any past coworkers? Using notes after the interview to complete and justify scores on a scorecard is essential.

## CODING CHALLENGE

Requiring take-home assignments—also referred to as coding challenges or interviewing homework—is a controversial topic. Take-homes are often a significant investment of time for candidates and are thus a significant source of candidate drop-off in the hiring funnel. It's not hard to imagine in-demand candidates being asked to do several take-homes, each of them requiring many hours or days of work, adding up to weeks of work. When facing those requests, it's understandable that candidates will prioritize the assignments for companies they are most excited about and/or have the most tractable assignments.

Despite these structural challenges, from a hiring manager's perspective, it's critical to have one. How can you hire a software engineer without having had them write code for you?

To summarize, there are three competing factors:

- **Establish Predictive Ability:** Employers' desire to have candidates actually produce code in a software engineering interview process to try and predict on-the-job performance.

- **Minimize Drop Off:** Employers' desire to have candidates actually complete coding assignments and not fall out in the funnel.

- **Improve Candidate Experience:** Candidates' desire to feel like their time is respected and the assigned tasks are reasonable. Ideally, a candidate should learn more about your company through this assignment and be even more excited about your opportunity.

## Predictive Ability

There are several styles of coding interview or assignment. Assignments range from take-home projects with a prompt, to using an online platform for programming exercises (also sometimes known as "code katas"), to live pair programming. Absent any empirical data about the predictive capability of these styles, I encourage you to design an exercise that looks as much like regular day-to-day work at your company as possible. If you don't do any pair programming at your company, then gauging how a candidate performs in an interview setting pair programming, intuitively, doesn't feel highly correlated/predictive. At the very least it's collecting tangential signals.

As a manager, your aim is to get the best out of the people you work with. With that in mind, try and recall the last time you were interviewed and exercise your empathy muscle when designing your coding assignment. Being interviewed is, for most, a very stressful process, and being asked to be creative or problem-solve in that scenario doesn't always bring out the best performance. Some ways to help candidates do their best work on a coding assignment are:

- Provide flexibility in choice of language/tools where possible.

- Allow for work to be done asynchronously (i.e., take-home instead of live coding).

- If you're indexing strongly on signals from the coding process such that take-homes aren't rich enough, consider asking the candidate to record themselves (via Loom or other similar tools) doing a part of the exercise.

- Be explicit about what you're looking for in the candidate's output. For example, if your scoring rubric measures how well they've documented their code, then ensure the prompt the candidate is given tells them to include documentation. Or if you plan to run the code, let the candidate know whether you'll just be evaluating correctness, or if other elements matter, such as performance, negative cases, etc.

## Candidate Experience and Drop-Off

Candidates are more likely to complete your take-home coding assignment if they find it interesting and easy to get started. The best assignments are topically related to your business and ideally expose the candidate to the kind of problems your company actually faces on a daily basis.

**Bad example:** You're a web SaaS platform, and you assign a candidate to do a challenge related to mobile phone development.

**Good example:** Your company integrates with many legacy third-party APIs, and your challenge is to build a limited integration with a Sandbox API with similar domain nouns/verbs to the real business.

Providing candidates with existing code repositories that have working build systems/tests to start with can save the candidate time bootstrapping a build themselves.

To be respectful of a candidate's time, I suggest providing a hard time limit for the take-home. The goal of a time limit is not to provide time pressure and force fast-paced delivery, but to ensure candidates are not overinvesting in the challenge and feel that the challenge is a reasonable request. To ensure candidates understand the time limit, you should

- Provide ample explanation of the time limit

- Ensure that the task is readily achievable in the time limit specified

Let candidates know how their submission will be evaluated. If your scoring rubric rates the candidate's README file, then let the candidate know they should spend time writing a README. If the code will be run—either live with the candidate or by an interviewer asynchronously—let them know that runtime will be judged. If you mostly care about architectural decisions and you're less concerned about runtime performance, let them know that, too, so they can spend time in the right way.

## TECHNICAL INTERVIEWS

As controversial and varied as the methodologies for take-home coding interviews are, technical interviews themselves are even more varied. In general, I encourage you to follow the same fundamentals: ensure you're collecting signals relevant to the actual job, and be respectful and considerate of candidates themselves.

The classic technical interview, practiced by many of the largest tech companies, involves some form of shared whiteboard experience where the candidate is asked to solve a technical problem in real time. The problems range from the academic, "sort an array with some special conditions," to high-level/hand-wavy architecture, "design a system to handle 100 million users posting news feed updates."

The classic interview approach must work for the big companies, as they continue to use it year after year, but I don't see how they work at a startup. They're often overly broad, or overly narrow, and thus difficult to score fairly. The academic questions are rarely correlated with the types of problems one solves on a daily basis on the job.

Most damning, they're not setting candidates up to be successful in the interview environment. After all, I'm sure there are very few engineers at the big companies writing array-sorting algorithms as part of their day job.

The methodology I outline in this chapter represents an alternative approach I've seen and used myself successfully in a startup environment.

## METHODOLOGY

What follows is a methodology I've used, derived from lessons in topgrading, to filter and hire senior software engineering candidates. In the spirit of topgrading, I call it the technical focus interview.

## Technical Focus Interview Guide

To find out where a candidate's strengths and weaknesses are, and how much that matters in the role you are hiring for, first you need to decide what topic areas matter for your role. You do this by creating a technical focus interview guide, which should include a list of anywhere from four to eight technical areas, and within each area a set of sample questions, best practice answers, and a scoring guide.

The sample answers and scoring guide are included to ensure fairness and uniformity in scoring across multiple interviewers and across candidates. You're trying to differentiate where any given candidate has gaps vs. true expertise, so your questions should be designed to elicit one of three kinds of answers: bad, good, and amazing. Thus, they should lend themselves to being scored as such. When it comes to scoring a question, to make the difference between a knowledge gap and true expertise obvious, I recommend that a bad answer gets a score of 0-2, a good answer gets a score of 3-6, and only an amazing answer gets between 7-10.

When I say a "bad" answer, I mean a response to the question that demonstrates either little to no experience or expertise with the topic at hand. A good answer demonstrates competency, maybe even a very high level of competency, in the topic. An amazing answer demonstrates not only competency but true understanding and intellectual depth on the topic. For example, if the question concerns how the candidate thinks about designing a unit test suite, and their answer is they've never thought about it, that's a 0 and you've found a gap. If their answer includes a description of some test suites they've designed and some justification for it, that's good, perhaps a 5 or 6. If their answer includes a full outline of test suite design philosophies and the pros and cons of each and how to apply them in different scenarios, now you're looking at real expertise and a 7-10 score.

In the spirit of giving candidates the best chance at success, I don't recommend scoring every question. Instead, provide a score on a topic area. This way you can try multiple questions within a topic, looking for areas of expertise with a candidate and scoring the net result for that topic.

Make no mistake, writing these questions, sample answers, and scoring guides is a lot of work. The good news is that any given question is useful across multiple roles and can be reused over a long period of time. In fact, I encourage you to maintain a central repository of questions (and associated sample answers/scoring guides). When it comes time to write the next technical focus interview guide, you'll find your job much easier by being able to reuse questions from the repository as appropriate.

See https://ctohb.com/templates for an example focus guide from my own question repository.

## Hiring Juniors vs. Seniors

The qualities you're looking for in a junior hire, with say one to two years of coding experience, should be very different from a senior hire with ten-plus years. The ideal junior hire should be curious, eager to learn, and have solid programming fundamentals to work in incremental feature development. A senior hire, by contrast, should come with not just programming fundamentals but deep thinking on architecture, opinions, and best practices across a wide range of tools and problems, and be able to develop trust that they can not only build incremental features but own and make good decisions in architecture for new greenfield projects. Since the key value these two types of roles offer is so different, it should follow that your interviews for them should be different.

For a senior hire, the focus interview—where you deeply explore the candidate's decision-making skills, understanding of concepts, and architectural know-how—is critical and should be weighed heavily. For a junior role, that knowledge deep-dive should be shorter, and weighed less heavily than a practical coding exercise.

## The Interview Itself

The senior software engineer technical focus interview is typically a sixty to ninety-minute conversation between the candidate and a lead interviewer, ideally with a primarily silent second interviewer on hand to take notes. Depending on the length of your focus guide and how many subjects you want to cover, you may consider splitting out the subjects into multiple focus interviews.

I emphasize that this interview should be conversational; you're looking to find out which areas of software engineering the candidate is most knowledgeable and passionate about, and in which areas they've either never been held accountable or have historically delegated. Doing this does not require brainteasers, pair programming, or any problem-solving. Simply ask!

Start the interview informally with some light conversation. After a minute or two, begin describing the agenda/plan for the meeting. Let the candidate know you have a document with an interview guide in it, and your goal is to get the candidate to discuss the topics in that guide over the next sixty to seventy-five minutes, leaving fifteen minutes at the end for them to ask you questions.

After the preamble you'll jump into the first section of the interview guide. Your goal in every section of the guide is not to ask every single question. You're looking first to determine which of the three categories the candidate falls into for that subject area—bad, good, or amazing—and then to narrow down a score from there. You should have a pretty good idea of where to categorize the candidate after the first question or two, then use follow-up questions to probe further to narrow in on a score.

If a candidate completely misses, or admits they aren't familiar with a topic, there is no need to keep going to every question; you've got your score and you can move on.

On the other hand, if a candidate nails the first question, they may well be a true expert in that area, but you likely won't be confident of their mastery until they've provided insightful answers to multiple questions across the subject. Typically, it takes more time and questioning to identify mastery than a lack of qualification.

Don't hesitate to politely cut off a candidate's answer and move on to the next category when you know you've heard enough. Your goal is to help the candidate demonstrate their skill and knowledge across all the topics that you've decided are important for this role and chosen to evaluate in this interview. Letting a candidate rabbit-hole and consume time on a single topic when you already have all the information you need for a score robs them of the opportunity to demonstrate their capabilities in other topics if you run out of time in the interview. It is your job, not the candidate's, to manage the pace of the interview.

## EXECUTIVE INTERVIEWS

By the time a candidate gets to an executive round interview, you should have already confirmed that they have the skills required in your job description and will be a suitable culture fit for your company. The executive interview, in most scenarios, is less about an executive screening a candidate and more a chance for the candidate to meet and ask questions of the executive.

If, however, the candidate is applying for a very senior role, or is going to be reporting directly to the executive, then it may be appropriate for this last interview to be longer or more thorough than simply candidate Q&A.

## REFERENCE CHECKS

With reference checks, you need to strike a balance between scheduling them early enough in the interview process to ensure that they don't create a bottleneck and not wasting time on reference checks for candidates who will not get offers. Keep in mind that candidates, rightfully, may be hesitant to provide references until they're at the end of a process to protect their own relationships with the references.

### TIMING

It follows then that reference checks almost always happen last in an interview process. To avoid having to delay an offer on completing reference checks, here are a few tips:

- Begin scheduling meetings, in parallel, with all references as soon as they are provided. Given their brief nature, the most efficient strategy may be able to call references without scheduling.

- Consider making an offer before completing references, but be clear with candidates that offer finalization is contingent on references coming back and meeting expectations. Reference checks, assuming you've done a good job with your filtering process up until this point, have a high success rate, so rarely will contingent offers have to be withdrawn due to failed reference interviews.

- Be flexible on who conducts reference interviews, as it does not have to be a member of technical staff. It does need to be somebody who is highly responsive to email and has considerable availability in their calendar to accommodate references.

## CONTENT

In general, reference interviews should be brief and respectful of the reference's time and willingness to help. Most reference interviews provide feedback ranging from neutral to enthusiastically positive. Very seldom will you receive overtly negative feedback, so your goal is to quickly differentiate between neutral and enthusiastically positive, confirm any strengths/weaknesses identified in the interview process, and move on. If you do get any overtly negative feedback in a reference interview, pay very close attention and try to get specific details on the criticism to bring back to the hiring manager.

Some sample questions for a reference interview:

- In what context did you work with [name of candidate]?
- Qualify how credible the reference is: have you managed many other engineers in your career?
- What were [name of candidate]'s biggest strengths?
- What were [name of candidate]'s biggest areas for improvement back then?
- How would you rate their job performance in that job on a 1-10 scale? What about their performance causes you to give that rating?
- [Name of candidate] mentioned that they struggled with _____ in that job. Can you tell me more about that?
- In what environment and under what management style would [name of candidate] be most successful?
- How does [name of candidate] manage conflict?
- Would you rehire [name of candidate] given the chance?

## MAKING AN OFFER

By the time you're ready to make somebody an offer you should have a strong opinion, based on the job description and feedback from your focus interviews, on the level at which you would be bringing in the candidate. From there it should be relatively straightforward to identify a salary/bonus/equity amount using your predefined leveling bands. (See 1.4.2 Compensation and Leveling, for more on this.)

Once you've calibrated your offer amounts, you should decide how to present the offer. Especially if your offer includes equity compensation, you should seriously consider providing a spreadsheet that provides context to the offer amounts. The value of a number of shares on its own is impossible for a candidate to assess. They need additional data points to value what you're offering, including numbers like total shares outstanding, share strike price, latest company valuation, etc.

I've prepared a sample candidate offer spreadsheet at ctohb.com/samples.

## PRESENTING THE OFFER

The moment when you present the offer is when you need to be in super sales mode. Ideally, you've been selling candidates all along the way so they're already very excited about the company and the opportunity for them. Regardless, this is a big deal for the candidate, so make sure to give the occasion the respect it deserves. Throughout the process of explaining the offer, remember to be especially upbeat, congratulate the candidate, and emphasize the fun you'll have and the great things you'll build together. It's also critical that you're transparent and outline all the key points of the offer upfront, especially anything they may not be expecting or used to, such as equity compensation or probation/trial periods.

I recommend making the offer in three parts: a phone call, an email, and a dinner. For the phone call, I suggest calling the candidate without prior scheduling. At this point you'll have already done a whole bunch of scheduling with the candidate, so there's no need to build up their anxiety further by scheduling yet another meeting. Alternatively, you could tell them in writing that you intend to extend an offer and schedule from there, but you lose the impact of being on the line with them when they get the news. I find it's just simpler to call the person and share the news all at once.

On the call, you should express excitement, convey the key points of the offer, and answer any initial questions. Explain that subsequent to the call you'll email them written materials to help provide context on the equity and, of course, a formal written offer letter will be coming from the company. And finally, if logistically possible, schedule a meal with the candidate to have a more personal, in-depth conversation.

# 1.3 Onboarding

Onboarding new engineers to the team, in most cases, doesn't strictly require a large investment from the team; a good engineer will "figure it out" eventually. That said, doing nothing will lead to a poor experience for your newest hire. It will slow down their time to productivity, and it may also make it harder to identify how well you've hired. Stated another way, good onboarding optimizes for three goals:

1. **It respects the employee:** A good onboarding experience helps a new hire to feel integrated into your company and culture and become productive as quickly as possible.

2. **It helps evaluate the quality of the hire:** Good onboarding provides structure for both the new employee and their manager, including clear goals that, when achieved, demonstrate that you've hired well for the role.

3. **It builds your culture:** Good onboarding emphasizes a culture of continuous improvement, helping to streamline the process for future hires and enhance the scalability of your overall processes.

There are many right ways to do this. What follows are some relatively simple and inexpensive techniques and practices that I've used myself. Feel free to expand on or deviate from these ideas.

## BOY SCOUT RULE: ONBOARDING

I encourage you to emphasize to your managers, your new employees, and in your onboarding documentation that successful onboarding is the shared responsibility of all members of your team(s), recent hires included. Depending on how often you are hiring, onboarding documentation has a tendency to get stale. If a new employee encounters something that is unclear, incorrect, or missing entirely from their materials, make it clear to them that you expect them to put in the effort to clarify and improve the documentation for the next person.

## Onboarding to the Team vs. the Company

There are elements of onboarding any engineer new to your company that should be consistent across all hires. This includes the high-level process, the emphasis on organizational culture, the types of documentation that new hires receive, and the structure of sharing documentation and setting onboarding milestones. You wouldn't want your frontend teams to have a rockstar-smooth onboarding process but your backend teams to be clueless. First impressions count, and onboarding is your opportunity to ensure that all team members get a great first experience of your organization and are introduced in a consistent way to your company's values and your team's best practices.

That's not to say that the nuts and bolts of onboarding will be identical across teams. You can and should have different materials for different teams when it makes sense, and every team and individual hire should have a customized onboarding plan and milestones.

## ONBOARDING DOCUMENTATION

There are two key elements of getting a new engineer onboarded: teaching them about your culture and best practices, and also giving them something to do by way of structure and instructions. I prefer to break these out into two written artifacts: "The Engineering Guidebook" and the "Welcome to [Your Company Name] Engineering, Day 1 Guide."

## THE ENGINEERING GUIDEBOOK

"The Engineering Guidebook" gathers in a single document all of the opinions, best practices, structural elements, and business operations of your engineering team. It should be the single source any engineer can rely on to learn about choices and decisions that are expected to be consistent across the engineering organization. Be deliberate and thoughtful about exactly what practices should remain uniform across the organization. The larger your team becomes, the more it will make sense for pieces of the team to develop their own specialized way of getting work done. That said, for most small/medium startups of, say, less than seventy-five to one hundred developers, there is a ton of value and efficiency to be unlocked by adhering to a healthy and consistent set of best practices.

The guidebook can take many forms, though my preference is as a slide deck/presentation. Some examples of practices your guidebook should outline:

- Software Engineering
  - Choice of programming languages
  - Opinions/requirements around CI/CD
  - Standards for naming (casing in code, casing in contracts)
  - Standards for data processing, protection, backup, security
  - Opinions on how to use source control (Git Flow, GitHub Flow)

- Opinions on testing (kinds, tools, how much to do)
- Standard patterns for frontend and backend authentication and authorization
- Wire protocol standards (REST, gRPC, GraphQL, etc.)
- Universal requirements (Do we support mobile, responsive, translation?)
- Certification frameworks and related training (e.g., PCI, SOC2, GDPR)
- Other coding logistics: accessing private repos, linting, static code analysis, commit message format/style.

- Engineering Process
  - Opinions on cadence/ceremonies (Agile, Kanban, retrospectives)
  - Opinions on technical documentation/specification requirements
  - Opinions on how to use the ticketing system (What's an epic? Do we use story points?)
  - Any metrics the team as a whole cares about (Are you measuring cycle time?)
  - How are production incidents handled (PagerDuty? RCA documents?)
  - How new technology gets incorporated into the stack
  - Process around bugs, tech debt.

- People Management
  - Expectations for how performance reviews are conducted, how individuals are evaluated/promoted
  - Expectations for contribution to onboarding/hiring processes.

The guidebook should be clearly labeled as a living document, with a well-defined process in place for proposing, getting feedback on, and incorporating changes to the guidebook. For example, I've used a Request for Comments (RFC) process for updates.

## WELCOME TO [YOUR COMPANY NAME] ENGINEERING, DAY 1 GUIDE

Distributing a "Day 1 Guide" is your opportunity to provide some structure for new employees, giving them a concrete list of things to do on their first day with your organization that will introduce them to the company culture, their teammates, your process, and your software stack. The Day 1 Guide should, of course, reference "The Engineering Guidebook" as required Day 1 reading. In addition, your Day 1 guide should cover the following:

- Instructions on how to get logins/access to required systems, including:
    - Source control
    - Ticket management
    - Any dev/stage/prod logging
    - Error tracking
    - Any design tools (Figma, Sketch)
    - Documentation/wiki (Confluence, Notion, etc.)
    - Internal communications (Slack, email)
- Information about company hardware (including whether new hires get to choose a laptop/phone), and expectations for using that hardware
- Instructions on how to set up a local development environment
- An introduction to the team and company organization chart: who their manager is, relevant cross-functional leaders, direct reports, and relevant VPs or executives
- Expectations around transparency and reaching out across the organization chart for help or escalation of concerns

- An introduction to the technical architecture
- Relevant books, blogs, and other written resources you encourage all team members to read

## ONBOARDING MILESTONES (AKA THE NINETY-DAY SCORECARD)

As discussed in the hiring chapter, hiring is very hard. Even the most thoughtful hiring processes will not achieve a 100 percent success rate. Said another way, mis-hires are inevitable.

The best way to handle the potential for unsuccessful hires is first to have the humility to acknowledge that your hiring process isn't perfect, and then to be thoughtful about how to measure the success of the new employees and take swift action to correct any mistakes. The process should be transparent upfront to new employees, clearly explaining expectations. Managers should work with new employees to make sure their role is a mutual fit, that the new employee is starting to feel at home in the role, and that they are delivering at a level commensurate with what they were hired for. At sixty or ninety days, it should be clear to both the new employee and the manager whether those expectations are being met.

If there is disagreement on whether the employee is being successful, that's a good sign that it's not working out, and you should consider relatively quickly whether there is another spot on the team where the new employee might be a better fit, or if both sides might be better off parting ways.

## THE SCORECARD

It is the responsibility of the manager of the new employee to identify and document measurable milestones for any new role *before* the new employee starts. On Day 1 the manager should walk through the milestones with the new employee, collect feedback, and collaborate on those milestones to ensure they are fair and clearly measurable. For some roles, these milestones may be easy and clear, such as in a support role measuring escalation tickets with ticket throughput. For other roles you may need to get more creative, for example, features delivered or story points closed. Regardless of the milestones you choose, the scorecard should do the following:

- Establish clear and transparent expectations between the manager and the new employee.

- Provide guidance for the new employee on what they will do and how they'll be measured in their first ninety days.

- Provide obvious criteria for meeting or not meeting the expectations of their role.

The scorecard doesn't have to be lengthy or highly nuanced. The key thing is that, whatever form it takes, after ninety days the employee and manager can look at the scorecard and agree on how the employee has performed and have a shared feeling of confidence on whether this is going to be a good long-term fit.

A quick word on the ninety-day length: ninety days is a commonly used timeframe for onboarding new employees, but it is not a hard rule. A thirty-day interval is generally too short in engineering, where there is a significant learning curve to mastering your technology, tools, and product. On the contrary, waiting a full performance cycle—e.g., six or twelve months— leaves a potentially poor fit in the role for too long, preventing them from getting the remediation they need to achieve productivity, and costing the company lost time and productivity. The right answer is likely in between, and the exact amount of time is up to you and your managers.

## HANDLING A SCORECARD FAILURE

If, after ninety days, the manager and the employee agree things aren't meeting expectations, or there isn't agreement on whether expectations are being met, something has to change. This doesn't mean you have to fire the new employee, but it does mean you have to do something. Consider the following options in this scenario:

- Is the problem the manager? Would this person be more successful on another team or with a different manager?

  ○ If you suspect this is the case, consider a lateral move before moving to termination.

- Is there a cultural misalignment?

  ○ Realigning an employee to your culture after a misalignment is identified is challenging and rarely successful. If you're concerned you may be in this scenario at ninety days, almost certainly the right option is to part ways, and more likely than not the candidate will be just as relieved as the manager.

- Is it a lack of experience or skill?

  ○ If you hired someone at a senior level but they're performing at mid-level, you have the option of attempting to down-level them. After all, it's unfair to other employees to keep this person on and pay them as a senior-level performer if they're not delivering at that level. Be warned, however, that down-leveling is very challenging. Unless expectations are very carefully managed, down-leveling will often result in bruised ego and ultimately prove unproductive or even toxic to your team.

## LETTING A NEW EMPLOYEE GO

In general, if it's not clear after ninety days that a hire is going to work out, it likely won't magically become better after 120 or 150 days, and it's best to let them go. You should terminate this employee the same as any other, with a full severance package and as much kindness as possible.

I encourage you to take full ownership of the mis-hire. If you hired them, take responsibility; it means your hiring process isn't perfect. Don't penalize the employee for it. An industry-standard severance package at a startup is four weeks' salary, benefits if you can extend them, and assistance finding another job in any way you're comfortable offering.

## ONBOARDING TIMELINE

Onboarding begins the second somebody agrees to work at your company and signs their offer letter. You should be thinking about how to make your new employee successful even before their first day. Not every new employee will be eager to spend their own time learning about the company or their role in advance of their start date, but depending on the task or what's offered, many will volunteer to do so.

I encourage you to send candidates your Day 1 Guide as well as your guidebook the day they sign their offer letter. If you have a company reading list, now is a good time to order those books and have them either shipped to the candidate or offer them in eBook/audiobook format. Most candidates aren't at all interested in reading/writing code before Day 1, but learning about your culture or reading high-caliber books on business/culture/engineering is rarely perceived as a burden. You shouldn't require this activity, but by making it available you'll likely get fairly healthy volunteer participation.

On their actual start date, the candidate should meet with their new manager first thing in the morning and check in. If they haven't read through the materials you sent them in advance of their arrival, set the expectation that they are to do so on Day 1. They should schedule follow-up time to review the ninety-day scorecard after the candidate has had a chance to review the introductory materials and set up their environment/logins. This is also a good time to reinforce the idea of continuous improvement and encourage the candidate to take ownership of any hiccups in their onboarding and contribute to improving the documentation and process for whoever follows them next onto the team.

# 1.4 Performance Management

One of the keys to improving employee morale and promoting a positive workplace culture is ensuring that everyone has a clear understanding of how they are perceived in the workplace and has reliable guidance on how to level up within the organization. The goal of any performance management system is to, as objectively and fairly as possible, provide that transparency and structure to employees. A bad performance management system will result in unwanted surprises or awkward and demotivating situations, while a strong performance management system motivates your team and encourages everybody to level up together.

Poor performance management often results in negative outcomes. Here are two examples:

- Person A is promoted and, as a result, Person B is surprised and feels skipped over. The situation worsens if the manager can't provide concrete justification for the decision when subsequently challenged by Person B, resulting in a sense of distrust, oversight, and cratered morale.

- Person X, having been at Level 4 for too long, feels exasperated and demoralized not knowing how to make it to Level 5 and get the associated raise.

Your performance management system should give everyone clarity on exactly where they stand, what they need to improve upon (and how), when they'll be evaluated, and how those evaluations are considered for promotions and compensation adjustments.

## COMPETENCY MATRIX AND LEVELING

Performance management and compensation design should not be done entirely by you, the technical leader. There are plenty of ways to make mistakes here that could expose your company to legal liability. These are easily avoided by ensuring that your HR lead is heavily involved in the process. In fact, ideally, your HR lead would do most of the blueprinting and lean on you only for help defining technical competencies. Regardless of who takes the lead, HR is your partner here.

## OVERVIEW

The core of a performance management system is a document, spreadsheet, or other workable artifact—here I'll call it a competency matrix (sometimes it's also called an impact matrix or an advancement plan)—that lists skills and areas of impact for each role. The competency matrix provides granularity, specificity, and expectations for what each skill/impact area looks like at various levels.

For example, an individual contributor software engineer's competency matrix may include a row for coding/feature output velocity. In a Level 1 to Level 5 system, the matrix would specify that for a Level 1 engineer, expectations on code velocity are X pull requests per week or the ability to close Y story points per sprint, whatever makes the most sense for your team. Ideally, each description is either directly measurable and specified quantitatively, or qualitatively tangible and interpreted in a consistent way by the team. The expectations for the remaining levels would increase incrementally and culminate in a very high bar for coding velocity at Level 5. In this way, with a complete competency matrix, any given team member should be able to rank themselves within each category and produce a set of rankings that would closely match those provided by their manager or peers.

Once you've got the descriptions for each level written out, all that's left is to publish a formula to summarize rankings of individual skills into a single job level. With that, you've got yourself a transparent, objective, measurable system any employee can use to understand their on-the-job performance and exactly where they can improve to level up. I provide a sample formula for this summation process in Performance Reviews, page 101.

Keep in mind that different roles should be evaluated for different contributions to the team and should have different (though perhaps overlapping) competency matrices. It is especially important to create a separate matrix for management as distinct from individual contributing engineers to encourage managers to grow their skills beyond coding.

## CREATING THE COMPETENCY MATRIX

The details of the competency matrix impact every member of the team, so it stands to reason that the team should be included in specifying those details. Referring to the "Team-Based Decisioning Models" section of Mini Management Frameworks, page 33, this is definitely a job for either the straw man or the codevelopment model.

I recommend the straw man model: Outline the key skills and impact areas you'd like to see for any given role and take a stab at filling out most of the competency matrix. Then introduce the idea to your tech team and let them know you'd like their input on how to flesh out that first draft. Set aside fixed time as a team and make it safe and encouraged to workshop the matrix together, perhaps using breakout groups to workshop individual categories.

Whatever structure you choose, make it explicit, provide at least a few hours of safeguarded time for working on it, and set a deadline by which to receive final feedback to incorporate and turn into a candidate final draft for the team.

Aim for at most five general categories, and no more than three areas within those categories. Any more than roughly fifteen skill/impact areas will make the matrix too unwieldy to use as an effective performance evaluation tool (and would certainly prove too cumbersome to collect timely team feedback).

Each level should have its rating system and performance expectations clearly described and/or can share a description with an adjacent level, where appropriate.

I've provided a sample advancement plan on my website for this book at ctohb.com/templates. Codeacademy.com also has a great template at ctohb.com/competencies.

## COMPENSATION AND LEVELING

I recommend tying compensation to the competency matrix leveling system, as doing so prioritizes two goals: fairness and incentivization for high performance.

Regarding fairness, if any two employees in the same role and level are compensated equally, then it stands to reason that the fairness of that compensation will depend on how fair the leveling is. If the team as a whole contributed to and believes in the fairness of the competency matrix, then by and large they will also believe that the compensation tied to that matrix is fair.

As for incentivizing high performance, tying compensation to leveling financially incentivizes everyone to level up. If the competency matrix is designed well and democratically, your team will focus on skills/areas of impact that actually help the business, which will earn them higher levels (and higher compensation) while also accelerating your team.

Translating levels into fair compensation is slightly more nuanced than most might assume. The easiest thing to do is create a transparent spreadsheet that says everyone at Level X gets paid $Y per year, but a few issues arise from such a strict system: cost of living adjustments (also known as local rates) and non-performance-based compensation bonuses.

GitLab published a great blog post explaining why they pay local rates (see ctohb.com/local. Their compensation calculator is also public at ctohb.com/gitlabcompcalc). That said, there's no one correct way to handle local rates, and you should consider whether or not paying them makes sense for your business. If it does, calculate those rates in a way that is both transparent and data-driven.

Having a performance level translate to a specific pay range, rather than an exact compensation amount, solves many compensation problems. Any given job will want to be calibrated to market rate, but how are market rates determined? Generally speaking, the tools and data that are available to determine a market rate will be somewhat imprecise, and at best give a range within 10–20 percent. The reason it's not more precise is simple: a software engineering role at your company is unlikely to be 100 percent identical in requirements to the same role at a different company. After all, your codebase and tooling aren't 100 percent the same.

Having a pay band also leaves room to increase compensation outside of the performance management system. Non-performance changes include tenure-based increases and inflation-based adjustments. You can also use pay bands as a rough stand-in and leave space for cost-of-living adjustments before your organization formalizes a more sophisticated local rate system.

## COMPETITIVE RATES & MARKET RATE DATA

So, you've designed your competency matrix and decided to translate levels into pay bands. Now, you just need to calculate your pay bands. This is an area you'll definitely want your HR lead partnering with you on closely to ensure you're meeting any regulatory requirements that may exist. Defining pay bands should be as data-driven as possible, and thanks to a handful of existing platforms (both paid and those that just require data-sharing), that data is relatively straightforward. Platforms like Pave, Option Impact by Advanced-HR, Levels.fyi, and Glassdoor can provide rich data sets that can be filtered to match the size/shape/stage of your company to determine a relevant pay band for a particular role.

## JOB TITLES

Many startup founders will tell you their organization is "very flat" and that "titles don't mean anything." That may actually be true from time to time in isolation, but it's the exception, not the norm. At the vast majority of companies, startups included, there are consistent trends in how titles are used. Assigning titles creates an expectation for level and scope of responsibility. Titles are also easily given and hard to take away, so it's worth being thoughtful and considerate about exactly what title you put on a job description or a promotion.

For non-executive roles, before you decide on titles I first encourage you to decide what your levels are using only numbers, e.g., Level 1, Level 2, etc., via a competency matrix (See Competency Matrix and Leveling, page 95). Once you know what to expect from each of those levels, you can map levels to titles. Don't be afraid to add a numeric suffix to titles as well; it's easier— and clearer—to use titles like "Junior Engineer 1" and "Junior Engineer 2" than it is to invent a new adjective that means "slightly more experienced than junior but not yet mid-level."

## ENGINEERING INDIVIDUAL CONTRIBUTOR TITLES

Titles for individual contributing engineers are pretty straightforward, using descriptive adjectives that convey seniority and size of responsibility. Most startups will use the primary three titles: junior, mid-level, and senior engineer. Beyond senior, phrases such as principal, fellow, and architect are often used, though they have a less consistent definition and hierarchy.

Senior individual contributors often have the informal title of tech lead. Tech lead implies that some of the individual contributor's time is spent on management-style responsibilities, but their primary responsibility is still doing engineering. Rarely is the notion of a tech lead something that is noted in a title on a résumé or organization chart; it's simply an added responsibility for more senior employees and is part of the expectation at that level of seniority. If a tech lead's primary output is management, not code, then they should be on a management track with a manager's expectations, title, training, coaching, etc.

## MANAGER TITLES

Management titling has more nuanced implications than individual contributors. The most common titles are software development manager (SDM) or software engineering manager (SEM), with appropriate seniority decorations—e.g., mid-level software engineering manager or senior software engineering manager. An SDM or SEM is usually responsible for a single team of engineers, who in turn work on a single feature or product.

The next level is typically a director of engineering. Directors are accountable for the performance, alignment, and output of multiple teams within single or highly adjacent products. In most organizations, a director is not expected to be a strategic role. In other words, a director isn't setting foundational technical direction or product strategy.

Beyond director is the role of vice president of engineering (VPE). There isn't a universal implementation of VPE. It varies from being the organizational lead of all engineers at the company (in place of a CTO) to being the strategic technical lead across multiple product areas. Sometimes the VPE reports to the CTO, and other times the CEO. What VPEs have in common, though, is the expectation of being technically very senior, experienced, and skilled at people management—a great communicator and strategic thinker.

## PERFORMANCE REVIEWS, SURVEYS, AND PROMOTIONS

Not all skill areas in a competency matrix can be evaluated quantitatively by a manager or spreadsheet, so every team needs a performance review process that can also collect qualitative feedback from managers and peers. The challenge is to collect qualitative feedback in such a way that it can be used to align with your leveling. In this chapter, I present a methodology I've used to collect feedback that ultimately results in a relatively easy-to-understand scoring system that can produce individual performance levels.

### REVIEW CADENCE

Performance reviews require a considerable amount of time, can be emotionally exhausting, and are very costly to your team, all of which push management to do them less often. The competing incentive is the fact that employees want tighter feedback loops and more opportunities for promotion. The balance is struck at scheduling reviews once every six or twelve months (more immediate feedback can and should be done with regular employee/manager 1:1 meetings). Remember, a sufficient amount of time between reviews is needed in order for individuals to grow and demonstrate that growth. Generally, six months is a safe lower bound that balances these concerns.

### REVIEWER SELECTION

The "who reviews whom" question has no easy answer. Many companies simply have the manager do the review, and that's it. While the manager's feedback is valuable, it can also leave too much room for bias and neglect the equally important perspective of peers and direct reports. The easiest (though slightly more costly) way to run a fair and comprehensive process is to have every employee receive multiple reviews that include these other perspectives, often called a 360 review.

Here I recommend using the straw man technique (see the "Team-Based Decisioning Models" section of Mini Management Frameworks, page 33): Each manager should create a list of direct reports and peers who have enough exposure to that team member to write a valuable review, then have a conversation with the employee and get feedback before finalizing the list. Managers should also keep track of how many reviews each employee is being asked to complete to keep the requests manageable.

## REVIEW QUESTIONS

Your questionnaire should mirror your competency matrix, and reviewers should be encouraged to make explicit references to the matrix.

The same set of questions can apply to each matrix category:

- What are some examples of this person excelling in this area?

- Where does this person demonstrate room for improvement in this area?

- What level do you think this person is performing at in this area?

Note that from an unconscious bias perspective, it's better to ask the reviewer to enumerate the examples before asking for a level. The alternative may encourage reviewers to choose a level, then cherry-pick examples to justify the level they've already chosen.

It may make sense to include some higher-level/softer questions at the end:

- How eager and excited are you to work with this person? (Scale: "Not excited at all" to "Very excited." This question is from Netflix's "Keeper Test" [ctohb.com/keeper])

- This person is currently at Level X. Do you feel they are ready for promotion to Level X+1?

- Are there any other strengths this person brings that you want to highlight?

- Are there any other areas for improvement that you want to highlight?

## REVIEW FORMAT

You can conduct reviews with or without the aid of a formal review tool (also known as performance or culture management tools, like Culture Amp and 15Five). Of course, a purpose-built tool will save time and scale this process quickly for larger teams. It's crucial to keep all individual feedback anonymous, with the exception of noting which scores came from management (we'll use those scores separately as a sanity check against peer reviews later in the process).

## RESULT CALCULATION

Once the reviews have been submitted, a set of scores should be reflected for each person in each category of the competency matrix, ideally broken out between scores from peers, direct reports, and managers. Here is an example matrix of scores:

| Level | 1 | 2 | 3 | 4 |
|---|---|---|---|---|
| # votes at this level across all categories | 2 | 6 | 8 | 4 |
| % of all votes | 10% (2 of 20) | 30% (6 of 20) | 40% (8 of 20) | 20% (4 of 20) |
| Cumulative score (see below) | 100% | 90% (20% [L4] + 40% [L3] + 30% [L2]) | 60% (20% [L4] + 40% [L3]) | 20% |

The challenge now is how to aggregate those scores into a final job level calculation. Some key considerations in this calculation:

- Protect the integrity of the process (e.g., that an employee didn't collude with their peers to artificially inflate or deflate anyone's scores)

- Ensure the formula is fair and can be calculated consistently

- Confirm that the manager's perspective of the employee's impact aligns with peer/subordinate feedback

- Decide whether all categories in the matrix are weighted equally or unequally.

Here's the method I recommend to determine a level: Assign the level at which the "Cumulative Score" is 66 percent or higher. The cumulative score for a given level is the percent of all scores that are at that level or higher. The lowest level will always have a cumulative score of 100 percent, Level 2 will be 100 percent minus the percentage of votes from Level 1. Level 3 is 100 percent minus the percentage from Level 2 and Level 1, and so on.

In the example above, the individual would be a Level 2. At Level 2, their cumulative score is 90 percent. Using the 66 percent rule, they are very close to a Level 3 (which is at 60 percent)—a mere two votes away. That they are so close can be used in coaching to encourage further improvement before promotion, or used to justify an adjustment within a pay band.

When you've completed your overall calculation, if you've managed to track a manager's scores separately, you can apply the same formula to the manager's scores in isolation and calculate the difference between the level resulting from the cumulative score of the manager's reviews and the level from the cumulative score of all peer reviews. A large delta there anything more than one level warrants close attention and additional review as it means the manager and peers have significantly different perspectives on an individual's performance. Or it might indicate some irregularity in the voting/scoring process.

## RESULT DISCUSSION

I encourage managers to provide performance review data ahead of an actual 1:1 performance review meeting to maximize the value of the meeting itself. It's best to give the individual the data and some time to process, so they can be fully engaged when the meeting occurs.

The agenda for the performance review meeting should be simple:

1. Discuss any strengths or weaknesses that were identified that are unexpected or otherwise not regularly covered in 1:1s.

2. Synthesize a small list of focus areas to work on before the next review

period. Many leaders advocate for a single focus area, but I've seen several individuals grow in more than one way during the given period, so two or three focus areas is a reasonable upper limit, as applicable.

3. Establish a schedule for the manager and employee to regularly check in on those focus areas and ensure there's advancement before the next review.

## COMPENSATION ADJUSTMENT ROLLOUT

At many companies, review feedback and compensation changes are handled at different times. I don't believe it is critical, or even advantageous, to discuss compensation changes in a performance review meeting, as this can distract from what can otherwise be a challenging but important discussion. The key thing is to set expectations for when compensation changes will be decided, communicated, and implemented before the performance review process, so they know what to expect before they walk into the meeting.

## PERFORMANCE IMPROVEMENT PLANS (PIPS)

Performance improvement plans, commonly referred to as PIPs, are a tool that provides structure to either improve an employee's performance or fire them. Some key aspects of PIPs:

- Everyone on your team should understand your company's PIP process.

    - Many people go into work with the same searing questions at the back of their minds: "Will I be fired today?" or "Am I doing well enough?"

    - Knowing that their company has a formal process for firing employees that includes an opportunity for correction can help reduce these anxieties.

- PIPs should only be used in a genuine attempt to address *and* improve underperformance, as they demand a significant effort from both the employee and the manager.

    - The manager should take time to thoughtfully complete the PIP document, making sure that it clearly articulates the underperformance, provides quantitative, clear evaluation criteria and structure wherever possible, and offers support and mentorship to help the individual improve.

- PIPs should allow a reasonable time period to demonstrate improvement—say, thirty days for individual contributors and sixty days for senior staff or managers.

- PIPs should always include a complete written version, not only to ensure clarity between employee and manager but also to provide documentation for HR/legal to have on record for any subsequent inquiries.

1.4 PERFORMANCE MANAGEMENT

There are a few situations in which you should bypass a PIP process and proceed straight to termination:

- Breaks in company policy, HR violations, inappropriate workplace behavior, etc., are not correctable with a PIP and should be met with zero tolerance.

- Certain skill gaps are not correctable with a PIP, such as general lack of good judgment on a certain topic, poor culture fit, or lack of experience in critical skill areas. This is most commonly a consideration for management or very senior staff positions where good skill judgment is critical to the role.

## CHANGING SEATS

Before developing a PIP or terminating an underperforming employee, it's worth asking the question of whether that person might be a better fit for a different team or role in the company. If the nature of the underperformance is skill-based, and the employee has skills that might be better applied in a different role, then changing teams can be very productive. If the underperformance is culture-based, then you'll likely find neither side has the motivation to attempt an internal transfer.

## Brilliant Jerks

A "brilliant jerk" is an industry-standard term used to describe an individual who is highly productive on their own, but whose presence hurts the morale or productivity of the people around them. They're often described as toxic personalities.

Due to their sometimes extraordinary individual productivity, choosing to fire a brilliant jerk can often feel difficult or wrong. The nearly universal recommendation is to fire them anyway. Each day that you, as a manager, allow toxic behavior to persist can increase your team's resentment toward you for allowing it to continue. There's no amount of individual productivity that makes up for the hit to company culture and to your credibility as a manager that retaining a toxic individual entails.

## FIRING

Your company should have a clear procedure for how to actually terminate an employee. My best advice: follow it. This is an area that, if handled incorrectly, can become a substantial liability to the company. Key considerations include:

- **Documentation:** Ensure you have sufficient documentation to justify the decision to let this individual go and to prove that the termination is based on performance or another for-cause reason.

- **Timing:** Once you've decided to let somebody go, do so as soon as possible. The common wisdom is that, after letting somebody go, managers typically worry less about whether or not that person should have been let go and more about whether they waited too long to do so. Mechanically, it doesn't make much of a difference what day of the week you decide is best to let somebody go, but if you are able to save it for the first day of the month instead of the last, you are offering the employee the benefit of an extra month on the company healthcare plan.

- **Witnesses:** Ensure that the manager and HR are present to witness the actual termination meeting. The meeting should be very short and to the point, and HR should answer most follow-up questions concerning termination logistics.

- **Offboarding:** Develop a plan in advance of termination for how and when to turn off the employee's access to company systems and recover any company hardware.

- **Severance:** Letting an employee go is most often just as much a failure of the company/management as it is the employee. Letting someone go is not a place to be spiteful or petty; that person has invested time and energy into your company, and you should do everything you can to set them up for success at their next role, including an industry-standard severance package (the range is somewhat broad, from a few weeks for an individual contributor up to two to three months for a senior executive, with packages also often factoring in tenure).

# 1.5 Team Makeup

The key difference in impact between junior and senior talent is the consistency with which they can reliably solve different kinds of problems. As engineers become more experienced, their judgment and decision-making improve on larger and larger surface areas. Similarly, you should expect that more senior talent will develop solutions that have fewer defects, last longer, and are more durable to requirements change along the way. That's not to say everyone has to be senior; in fact, it's rare that a majority of projects involve architecting brand-new greenfield solutions. The right blend for any given team considers the types of work to be done and staffs the team thoughtfully as a result.

## SENIORITY MAKEUP

Your team should be more heavily weighted with senior engineering talent if your codebase

- is very new, requiring lots of architecture and foundational contract creation;

- is very old, poorly maintained, or poorly thought up and considered difficult to work in—in short, a brownfield codebase;

- is meaningfully changing in requirements, especially if new requirements do not look very much like old requirements;

- is using new tools, techniques, or patterns that require validation for your problem;

- requires establishing new patterns/ways of doing work, especially with ecosystems that don't provide tight guardrails that encourage healthy patterns.

## TECHNICAL SPECIALIZATION

On Day 1 of most startups, the team will consist of a small handful of engineers, typically two or three. Having a team of three leaves limited opportunity for specialization. There are twenty categories of technical work to do and only three people, so by the pigeonhole principle, at least one person and more likely all three will be doing many types of technical work. Said another way, early on at your company, everyone is expected to wear many technical hats. As your company grows and you add more people to the team, you and your employees will find more opportunities for specialization.

So, you've raised a round of funding and you're looking to expand your team for the first time. How do you decide whether you need frontend engineers, backend engineers, DevOps engineers, etc.? Here are some general guidelines:

- **Listen to your team:** The people currently doing engineering are very likely to be vocal about where the biggest sources of inefficiency are, and where the most help is needed. Your job as a manager is to take in that perspective and extrapolate going forward. Is the team pointing out a problem that will disappear in two months, in which case hiring somebody wouldn't be appropriate? Or is the issue systemic in nature and likely to continue for the long haul?

- **Look for factors that are hurting produ-ctivity:** If your team is mostly frontend engineers and you're struggling with backend reliability, then that should be a sign that you need backend or DevOps engineering help. This same principle applies to testing, developer experience, etc.

- **Specialize with scale:** Until your team is north of a dozen people, chances are high that you're better off with a team of primarily generalists.

Here are some rough numbers for team composition based on startup experience:

- Team size 1–5
  - Your team is all generalists, specialized at most between frontend, backend, and mobile.

- Team size 5–15
  - Your team is specialized by product or general skill area such as backend, frontend architecture, frontend design, DevOps, and testing.
  - You'll likely want to start thinking about dedicated resources in testing and DevOps when you've grown to (or past) fifteen engineers.

- Team size 15–30
  - You should have real specialization by this point and be hiring only people with expertise in a subfield of software engineering.
  - At this point, any inefficiencies in "how work gets done" are likely to start getting very expensive across the team, so make sure you're investing either headcount or time in ensuring that developers are able to get work done, their tools work, and operational logistics are streamlined.

- Team size 30-plus
  - At this stage there are many methodologies for breaking out teams into smaller units to ensure work stays efficient. If you have multiple product lines, aligning team members with specific product lines is a fairly natural place to start organizing.
  - Many companies at this stage use a concept of "pods," where a pod has a focus area and is made up of a diverse/cross-functional team capable of independently executing tasks in that area.

## PROJECT MAINTENANCE: THE "TWO CREWS" PHILOSOPHY

If you are shipping end-user software, your engineering team has to strike a balance between doing new work and handling support tickets that come in from active customers. Left unchecked, the need to handle support tickets can become a major distraction to the team, hurting efficiency, draining morale, and burning out your best people. There are many right answers to solving this problem; the important thing is that you recognize its effect on your team and architect a solution to help them be productive and drive great customer outcomes.

Microsoft has published a great article on this topic titled "Building productive teams" (ctohb.com/teams) describing what they call the "two crews model." The two crews model outlines a feature crew and a customer crew. The feature crew focuses on the future, building new features. The customer crew focuses on the present, working on active customer issues, diagnosing bugs, and prioritizing site health.

Other names for customer crew might be a maintenance team, or a "Tier 2" support team (where "Tier 1" is your non-technical customer support staff).

Splitting maintenance work off into its own team has many benefits:

- It allows for a dedicated team to monitor the customer queue at all times, triaging and resolving anything important and urgent.

- It allows your feature team to remain 100 percent focused on the future, undistracted by customer support work.

- It allows for developing specialization within the customer crew, building tooling and expertise at handling issues, making issues less expensive to handle over time.

- It provides another career path for individual engineers, especially junior engineers, to learn and level up on your team.

The first question I get asked about the two crews approach is: how long does somebody stay in the customer crew? There are four approaches to determining customer crew tenure:

- Make the customer crew a permanent, distinct team or department. You have published job descriptions for engineers focusing on support and debugging. Note that for many engineers, a job focused only on debugging may sound undesirable. To me, a job description that emphasizes data entry or accounting sounds very unpleasant, and yet there are many people who enjoy and even pursue those jobs. Don't assume that just because you wouldn't do that job, there aren't others who might be excited by the prospect. In particular, working on a customer crew exposes an engineer to a huge amount of code, often offers opportunities to talk to customers, and involves less product-driven deadline pressure—all things that might appeal to the right candidate.

- Create an explicitly discussed career trajectory for engineers to start on the customer crew and, after a period of time (usually twelve-plus months), transfer to the feature crew.

- Engineers rotate between the crews on a regular basis. The Microsoft blog post referenced above recommends swapping some team members between the two crews every week.

- Define the customer crew as a temporary team. This can mean either that the customer crew itself doesn't exist full-time (perhaps for only one week per month), or that team members are constantly rotating between the customer and feature crews.

I recommend creating a dedicated, permanent customer crew only for teams or products where customer issues are costly enough for the team to warrant it. If you're in a high-support business, a dedicated customer crew can be a force multiplier for both engineering productivity and customer satisfaction.

## TEAM ORGANIZATION

In general, you'll find technical organization charts organized in one of two ways: functional organization and product organization. A functional group is organized around the type of work team members do, such as frontend engineering, testing, or a particular internal service. Product groupings, sometimes called business units, are organized around a particular business-related/product focus, such as the enterprise core application team or the consumer mobile app team. How you choose to organize your team can have a significant impact on team collaboration, productivity, and morale. Product-organized teams, often called pods, are the right answer most of the time.

When you're designing an organization chart you should consider what you're optimizing for. For a startup, the primary goal of an organization chart is to ensure that different people who need to collaborate closely with one another are enabled and encouraged to do so by the organizational structure. The best way to achieve that is to have all the people who directly contribute to the feasibility and success of a product be organized together, to hold them accountable to a common set of goals, and to develop a shared sense of ownership over that product.

When your team is small, and you have just one product, the question of how to organize is moot—it's one cross-functional team all working on the same product. By the time your team has grown to 12 or more people, you'll need to start being more deliberate about defining what a pod is, and finding a method that is easy to understand and grounded in your product reality, before breaking your team out into pods.

The advantages of pods are greater team cohesion, autonomy owner-ship, accountability, and overall execution velocity. This approach is not without tradeoffs, however. Having a long-lived group of engineers work on one product can create knowledge silos. As organizations scale, it's also more likely for a product team to make architectural decisions that might optimize locally and lead to duplicate work or inefficient use of compute resources. If you anticipate and plan for these issues arising, the pain they induce—when well-managed—will be far outweighed by the benefits of autonomous, high-performing pods.

## MANAGING REMOTE TEAMS

There are a sufficient number of successful 100 percent remote software engineering teams that it is incontrovertible that remote organizations can work. That's not to say all remote teams are successful, or that it's necessarily easy to build an entirely remote culture. I've spent nearly a decade managing remote teams. Below are some recommendations that should apply to most remote management scenarios.

### DOCUMENTATION

Being remote means that there's nobody sitting next to you to answer questions, but that doesn't mean the questions go away. Those questions still get asked, only now social context is lost and so perhaps the question goes unanswered for a while. Or, rather than holding questions until the other person takes a break, now they get asked immediately, prompting various kinds of notifications and distracting from focus work. Having a robust set of internal documentation with an effective search feature can speed up time-to-answer and reduce the number of one-on-one context switches that become barriers to getting work done.

### ASYNCHRONOUS WORK

A great way to turn remote work into an asset rather than a liability is to lean into asynchronous working practices. A strong asynchronous culture reduces the burden of time zone mismatches and reduces the amount of time spent in remote meetings/dealing with remote context switches. (See

Benefits of Overcommunication, page 20, for more on asynchronous communication and the value of asynchronous work.)

## IN-PERSON MEETUPS

As useful as they are, video calls are no substitute for sitting down and having a meal as a team. The bonds that are formed by in-person meetings tend to endure over a long period of time, so an investment in even infrequent in-person meetings can improve the quality of social relationships between team members for months. As a general rule, it's healthy for a team to meet in person once per quarter to maintain these relationships and minimize remote social frustration.

## TIME ZONE OVERLAP

My overall recommendation is for teams that are working on the same project to have a minimum of four working hours of overlap. That leaves a sufficient window for any regularly scheduled meetings and an opportunity for ad-hoc conversation and questions.

## CREATE SOCIAL OPPORTUNITIES

In general, people's default mode with video calls is to multitask during the call and then get off the call as fast as possible. Once a work conversation is over, everyone hangs up. That isn't how people interact in person; for example, the meeting ends and then you talk about sports in the hallway when walking back to your desks. That bit of social time before/after meetings is a valuable way for people to build relationships and trust, and it won't happen unless the leadership and culture actively support it. A cheap and easy way to do that on a regular basis is to ask a lighthearted, round-the-room, icebreaker style question on a regular basis, such as "What's one bit of good news personally, and professionally, you can share?"

You can support remote social building with remote happy hours, or virtual team dinners and social activities. Post-COVID-19, there are many online social facilitators who run remote events ranging from digital casino nights to virtual escape rooms.

## CAMERA ON

Depending on which article you read, 70–90 percent of communication is nonverbal. Using a webcam during a video call doesn't replace all of that 70 percent, but it is unquestionably an improvement over having no video at all. Since webcams are so cheap now, there's really no justification for not having that additional social communication bandwidth within your company. The common objection is that employees are worried that others may judge their appearance on camera. If that's a concern you are facing, I encourage you to walk through the business justification for wanting as high-quality communication as possible in a remote setting, and have a zero-tolerance policy for any employee who makes inappropriate remarks on another's appearance. It can also be helpful to create a space for people to do whatever they feel appropriate to get themselves ready, such as allowing/encouraging background blurs, and occasional video-off to deal with something in reality or to tidy up.

## RECORDING MEETINGS

Recorded meetings provide a great way to allow employees to get up to speed on a topic without requiring a work stoppage for a calendared meeting. In general, you'll find that very few employees or candidates are opposed to the idea of recording video calls. Recordings are also a great way to expose more people to some content than is perhaps comfortable in the moment. For example, you may want a hiring team of four or five people to watch an interview with a candidate, but having five people in the room at the time may be intimidating. Making a recording of a 1:1 interview is an excellent way to ensure everyone has the opportunity to evaluate the candidate without creating an uncomfortable or unfair situation by overloading the interview meeting itself.

# 1.6 Leadership Responsibilities

As an executive, your leadership responsibilities extend beyond the technical components of developing and growing an engineering team. You should be looking to help the company be successful as a whole, with a particular bent toward how technology contributes to that success. Doing that means keeping an eye on how technology is working with the rest of the company by facilitating healthy collaboration with other teams, both in-house and external, as well as putting into place good process and management practices surrounding technology and product development.

## PRODUCT AND DESIGN TEAMS

It's your responsibility as a technical leader to ensure that your engineering team is working efficiently with the product and design teams, even if those teams report to somebody else. When designing this process, as a general rule, throwing things over walls between groups isn't efficient. Good interaction between product, engineering, and design teams requires empathy and understanding. What does the other team do, what challenges do they face, and how can you and your team make their lives easier? Below I'll provide a little background on these other functions and some concrete suggestions on how to work together efficiently.

### DESIGN SYSTEMS

Design teams would ideally like their work to be implemented faithfully, pixel-perfect, by the software engineering team. Absent any sort of structure or set of constraints, actually achieving pixel perfection is expensive or even impossible; however, a bit of shared understanding and a design system can make the task dramatically cheaper.

A design system is a set of standards for managing design at scale using reusable components and patterns. Large companies tend to create their own design systems. Atlassian, for example, makes theirs available publicly (ctohb.com/design). As a small startup, innovating on design systems is likely not key to your success, so it follows that you should use an off-the-shelf design system. Nowadays you can choose from a plethora of off-the-shelf systems with rich feature sets and a variety of aesthetic styles that, more likely than not, can be customized to match your brand.

Not only do design systems provide a time-saving set of guardrails and components used by designers, they often come with out-of-the-box support for various frontend languages and frameworks. Material Design, for example, has a published design system in Figma (ctohb.com/figma), as well as a set of JavaScript react components (mui.com) and angular components (material.angular.io).

By adopting a system like Material (or AntD, Chakra UI, Blueprint, Bootstrap, Semantic UI, etc.) you not only get a suite of prebuilt technical components but you also get a system that integrates neatly with designer tools. By integrating the same system with the tools of both engineers and designers, you'll ensure that what your designers create will map cleanly to the components available to engineers. This cuts down or even eliminates the need for engineering to do custom styling or frontend UI, and makes it easy to match a design down to the pixel.

Beyond the efficiency gained by having consistency between design and engineering, most design system component implementations also take into account or automatically solve for other design priorities, such as accessibility (both for screen readers and color contrast management for the colorblind), adherence to UI standards, and even out-of-the-box dark mode support.

## PRDS AND SPECS

A Product Requirements Document (PRD), sometimes also called a product specification, or just a spec, is an essential part of the product development process. Note that a product spec has a different purpose and is a distinct document from a technical spec (see Technical Planning and Specifications, page 164) There are many methodologies and templates for PRDs. Sources like lennysnewsletter.com regularly catalog some of the most common and thorough ones. PRDs have a shared purpose, which is to describe the problem background as well as the "why" that justifies a project or feature. PRDs often include lists of requirements that need to be met to meet an objective. Most PRDs leave the "how" of a feature to a technical spec.

A PRD, like a technical spec, is a living document. As your team learns more about the problem, or as factors in the outside world change, these documents can and should change and be updated to match. I encourage you and your team to use these documents as a continually updated source of truth to document your considerations and ultimate decisions made during the product development process.

## EPD

EPD is an industry acronym for Engineering Product and Design. The implication is that all three departments are essential to the product development lifecycle and need a healthy way of working together to produce great results. From the business's perspective, all three departments together are responsible for producing a product the customers love, so it's helpful to have a single person with a single set of business goals setting the direction for all three units.

# Product vs. Project Management

Product and project management are industry terms with distinct meanings. A product manager is accountable for the design and creation of the product as well as the key performance indicators (KPIs) the product should meet for the business. Melissa Perri's *Escaping the Build Trap* is a phenomenal resource that dives deeply into the role and impact a great product manager can have on your organization. A project manager is accountable for guiding the internal organization of the team, managing internal communication, and adhering to the roadmap and deadlines.

Early on in your startup, as CTO you may be filling both of these roles. Very early in your hiring roadmap you should plan to have a great product manager who can take some of these responsibilities from you. Some product managers excel at project management, while others don't find joy in it and therefore don't put time and attention into it. Arguably, early on at your startup, it's okay either way; with a small team, the consequences of lax project management are minimal. However, as you get larger, formalizing project management becomes more important, and if your product manager isn't filling the role, you should aim to augment them with a project manager.

My general recommendation is to formally delegate project management when EPD has grown to around twenty people. That will mean formally assigning yourself that role, having the product manager do it, or hiring a dedicated project manager. You'll want to be involved early on in setting up project management processes, ensure that the mechanisms being put in place for project management support the kind of culture you're looking to build, and are empathetic to all parties involved.

## MANAGING MANAGERS AND MANAGER TRAINING

There's an industry expression that "your company is ultimately run by your middle managers." The implication is that, despite whatever strategies and processes executives put in place, it's the middle managers who ultimately have the highest impact on the quantity and quality of output. Middle managers hire individual contributors, set their day-to-day objectives, and hold them accountable for quality standards. The best middle managers are mini executives, focused on culture, building collaborative teams, and working to enable them to do their best work. It follows then that, as an executive, you should put a lot of effort into hiring, managing, and training those middle managers.

The complicated topic of training managers deserves an entire book on its own, and it's a skill that takes time to master. That said, the top two lessons I can offer you that will provide leverage to all other skills here is to set an example yourself and build a culture of continuous management learning. The minute you hire or promote somebody into management you should make it clear that your expectation is that they will commit to putting time and effort into refining their craft of management. You'll go out of your way to make that easy for them by including management training in their personal goals and development plan, providing them resources to level up on management skills, helping them work through management problems, and teaching them everything you know.

Management training doesn't have to be over-the-top burdensome and expensive. If budgets permit, I highly recommend hiring outside management coaches for your managers. An internal manager monthly book reading/review can also be effective at kickstarting the continuous development flywheel.

## FINANCES AND BUDGETING

Part of your role is likely shouldering accountability for the present and future cost of the software engineering department (and sometimes design and product departments). As a responsible steward of that budget, you should know how much was spent on various items in the past, and how much your company as a whole has allocated in the future. Most importantly, you'll need a plan to justify spending that allocation wisely.

In general, you'll find the two largest line items in a technical department are people (payroll) and infrastructure/SaaS. Keep in mind that the actual cash cost of an employee is higher than just their salary, as it will include benefits and payroll taxes. A good rule of thumb is that the cash cost of an employee is 20 percent above their salary; this percentage is referred to as the burden rate.

## THE BUDGET

Most finance teams use sophisticated accounting and budgeting software to manage the company's books. If not, they'll have a company-wide spreadsheet that's far larger and more complex than you need as CTO. In my experience, finance departments are not usually willing to let people outside of finance make changes to the core budgeting system, so unless they give you something to start with, it's on you to make a financial model for your department.

Given that your department's costs are fairly predictable, and centralized in a few line items, the model you make doesn't have to be very sophisticated. My recommendation is that you maintain a spreadsheet that includes the following:

- Payroll tab

- SaaS/Costs of Goods Sold (CoGS) tab

- Infrastructure tab

- "Other" tab (including travel, hardware)

- Summary tab

You can find a sample technical department budget spreadsheet on ctohb.com/templates that will get you most of the way there on the actual modeling.

## WORKING WITH YOUR CFO

If your company is like most startups, you'll be the most expensive department, and your CFO should be well aware of that. Some things to consider that are helpful for you and will make your CFO your best friend:

- Help your CFO know how money is—and will be—spent. Avoid surprises wherever possible. Provide guidance for things like hardware cost, travel/conference cost, and cloud cost upfront.

- Maintain a budget for your department and keep it up to date with changes in your forecast.

- Update your budget regularly with actuals from the finance department and ensure the delta between forecast and actual is understood and managed.

- Establish a plan for hiring and include estimated salaries.

- SaaS bills are often a burden to track. Consider either using a credit card statement analysis tool (i.e., a SaaS Management Platform, aka SMP) or hiring an assistant to regularly categorize and reconcile these expenses with your budget.

- Finance departments often care a lot about cost attribution to differentiate; for example, costs that are part of Costs of Goods Sold (COGS). Indicating in your budget a very coarse-grained "why" for each line item can win you friends in finance.

## MEASURING ENGINEERING VELOCITY/HEALTH

I have yet to encounter a technical team or leader who has managed to consistently and usefully quantify actual engineering output. This includes measuring velocity as the sum of estimates of completed tasks. (See the "Estimates" section of Workflow, page 160, for a discussion on the unreliability of technical estimates.)

I have, however, seen many companies effectively measure engineering health and contributing factors to engineering velocity—namely, cycle time and work time allocation.

### CYCLE TIME

Cycle time is a measurement of how long it takes to go from idea to shipped feature, and is often broken down into these sub-milestones:

- Time spent coding
- Time to start a code review
- Time until code is approved
- Time to deployed code

In general, low-cycle teams are more efficient and able to iterate, innovate, and deliver value to customers faster. There are many tools that facilitate measuring cycle time, including LinearB (linearb.io) and Code Climate (codeclimate.com). LinearB has published a set of benchmarks, using data from thousands of engineering teams, on metrics associated with cycle time.

### WORK TIME ALLOCATION

The idea of measuring work time allocation is that, while measuring how much work is done is difficult, it's comparatively easy to measure what types of work team members are spending their time on. This resulting information is directionally useful. For example, if a team is spending the majority of its time addressing bugs, then it's a good hypothesis that improving software quality and bringing down that time percentage will result in more time allocated to developing new features, and thus an overall improvement in health and velocity.

Actually measuring work time allocation can be done in a semi-automated way by pulling reports from ticket systems, or it can be measured with regular lightweight pulse surveys to the team.

## FUNDRAISING AND DUE DILIGENCE

Generally speaking, as CTO, your role in fundraising and due diligence is fairly minimal. At most startups, the CEO and perhaps the CFO do the lion's share of that work. Your involvement likely comes toward the end of the process as investors do due diligence on the company. Many (though sadly not all) of the requests made in due diligence are for information that a well-organized engineering team already maintains as part of doing business. Keep an eye on on the following, and be ready to produce for due diligence:

- Organization chart

- Department budget

- Full description of all products engineering has created and maintains

- Engineering roadmaps (usually they're looking for short/medium-term roadmaps)

- A list of major areas of tech debt, what I've labeled a "tech debt balance sheet" (see Tech Debt, page 145)

- High-level system architecture diagrams

- Full description of how software is distributed and updated, either as SaaS or as versioned desktop/mobile software

- A high-level description of systems, how they're hosting, and your security practices

- Information about software licensing, including code scans of company code confirming no license violations or unlicensed proprietary software

It's not uncommon for an investor to hire a third-party firm to conduct a technical diligence audit. These audits may involve interviews or meetings with you and perhaps a few other senior members of the team. Be prepared to discuss your engineering process, assess the general productivity of the team, and do a code walkthrough of parts of your system.

My advice is to be candid with these auditors. They've looked at a lot of tech companies and are well aware that all engineering teams have debt and parts of the system that teams are more proud of than others. The more your investors know about your strengths and weaknesses, the better they can support and hold your team accountable for improving the weaknesses going forward.

## VENDOR MANAGEMENT

In general, the responsibility for sourcing, negotiating with, and managing third-party technical vendors will fall to you as the CTO. For most, this is an unenjoyable but necessary part of the job, and consequently, it doesn't get much thought. Performing this responsibility well, however, can provide significant cost savings for a business. Here, I'll walk you step by step through a typical SaaS negotiation/signing process and provide some tips for how to add efficiency and save cost.

### SELF-SERVICE SIGNUP TOOLS

Typically, either you or a member of your engineering team will highlight a need for a type of tool, and if it's one of your engineers or managers they'll ask either for you to approve the expenditure or for you to sign up for the tool. Many tools are inconsequential in cost and have trivial self-service signup flows. I recommend you work with your budget and finance team and set a threshold below which your managers are authorized to simply sign up for the tool independently. For tools that are above the cost threshold or don't have self-service signup, you'll need to enter into a discovery and negotiation process with an enterprise vendor, which typically has four steps.

### ENTERPRISE TOOLING

You're now facing an enterprise sales process. Before reaching out to the vendor's sales team, be sure that this particular company is the one best suited to solve your problem. In most instances, I recommend starting a spreadsheet, doing some diligence on all the vendors in the space, and filtering down to a top two or three. Even if one of them is by far your preferred choice, it doesn't hurt to have some deeper context on the space and for negotiating knowledge/leverage/BATNA (best alternative to a negotiated agreement).

## Sales Qualification

When you first reach out to an enterprise vendor you'll almost certainly enter what is called a sales qualification process. At this step, especially as a technical executive, your needs are not yet aligned with the vendor. You're probably looking for pricing, a contract, and the shortest path to getting started. The vendor is looking to make sure you're their target customer and are likely to sign up and not churn for at least a few years.

Most SaaS sales companies will have frontline sales representatives take the initial phone call, and their primary objective is to learn about your company and see if you fit their profile. They might not have much technical knowledge and often they won't be able to discuss pricing with you. As a result, you're not likely to get much value from this first meeting. My advice is to either delegate these intro meetings or try and get the sales qualification questions from the rep via email and answer them sufficiently to skip the intro meeting altogether.

## Negotiation

Once the vendor has validated that you fit the mold of their target customer, they'll schedule a second meeting with more senior resources on their side. Typically, this would be a sales manager or perhaps a technical sales representative. This is the stage at which you'll start to get answers to more of the technical questions you have about the solution, and you'll get some transparency into the pricing models the vendor is authorized to use.

Here are some general negotiating tips:

- Keep in mind that, at the end of the day, a salesperson's job is to sell you the product, so you're on the same team when it comes to landing on terms that are mutually agreeable. The more transparent you can be about what matters to you, the better they'll be able to craft a sales agreement that meets those needs.

- Don't undervalue factors other than total cost, such as total contract length (longer contracts should come with steep discounts), payment frequency, payment terms (e.g., net 30, net 90), or what happens to contracts in the event of a change in control of either company.

- In general, look for contracts that grow as you grow. Ideally, the initial cost is low and grows over time as the tool is used more heavily and provides more value. Encouraging a "we grow together" mindset can help reduce those initial costs.

- Keep your finance and compliance teams in the loop. If your CFO is great at negotiating, let them handle this part of the process.

- If your total SaaS budgets are large or you're negotiating a lot of these deals, consider using a third-party negotiator, such as Vendr. Often these negotiators will charge based on how much they save you, and they have data from many more contracts than you do to understand pricing.

- Be aware that end-of-month/quarter quotas are real and discounts around that time are very common.

## Signing

Once you've agreed on terms and exchanged paperwork, the next step is to find out who the authorized signers are for your company (assuming you're one of them), get the documentation signed, and keep it organized. Do not lose or misplace these contracts as they'll be useful for future negotiations or due diligence. Ensure you're tracking the costs in your budgets or with your SaaS management platform (SMP).

## Post-Sales

After the deal is signed you will likely be handed off to a different representative at your vendor, someone whose title is similar to either post-sales support or customer service manager (CSM). These individuals are incentivized by, measured by, and focused on customer retention or product upsells. They're knowledgeable about the product, and at least somewhat technical. Going forward, they'll serve as your advocate for new features and getting defects resolved.

# 1.7 Which Type of Startup CTO Are You?

Whether you're the CTO, a CEO playing the role of CTO, or a founder hoping to hire a CTO, it's helpful to have a clear understanding of what exactly it is a CTO does in a startup, and how that role differs from executive and leadership roles in more established companies. As with most things, the answer depends on context and will change over time. Calvin French-Owen has a great article (ctohb.com/founder2cto) breaking down the CTO into four archetypes: People Leader, Architect, R&D, and Marketing/Consumer-facing. I like this breakdown and will refine it a bit here to three types:

- Tech-Focused

- People-Focused

- Externally Focused

## The Tech-Focused CTO
### *AKA The Chief Architect*

The tech-focused CTO may also be the "office of the CTO," leading an internal technical skunkworks whose primary output is forward-thinking strategy, architecture, and sometimes proof-of-concept implementation on how to help the business down the road. This CTO will have fewer reports, with the bulk of the engineering organization reporting to a separate vice president of engineering. In this case, it's not uncommon for the vice president of engineering (VPE) to report to somebody other than the CTO—most commonly, directly to a CEO or to a chief product officer (CPO).

The internal tech-focused CTO may also be the chief technical process architect, setting up tools, systems, and processes for how technical work gets done.

As an internal tech-focused CTO, you may also function as a product manager if your company's product is highly technical in nature (i.e., developer tools, API-as-a-service, etc.)

## The People-Focused CTO
### AKA the VP of Engineering (VPE)

A typical startup will not have both a VPE and a CTO, and so it often falls on the CTO to fill the VPE role. This is often also the hardest role for a cofounder CTO to fill, as the responsibilities of the day one technical cofounder don't much overlap with the responsibilities of the internally people-focused technical leader.

The people-focused CTO is responsible for setting internal technical culture, the hiring process, and overseeing internal processes. This CTO spends much of their time actually managing either independent contributors or other technical managers. This is the most critical of the three focus areas to get right. If a company isn't hiring well, or its technical staff is poorly managed, unmotivated, unfocused, or not aligned, it can impact productivity, and even lead to bad decision-making that will hurt the organization in the long term.

## The Externally Focused CTO
### AKA The Head of Technical Sales/Marketing

This is likely the least common focus for a startup CTO, but no less critical at the right time or place. Most often, you see this CTO at companies that build products for a technical audience—developer tools, for example. These CTOs spend lots of time writing blog articles or speaking at conferences. Perhaps they are brought into sales meetings to act as an executive technical representative to close large deals. Note that building a brand around the technical team not only has a positive effect on product sales, but also can be a great recruiting tool and can reduce your time and cost of hires.

This is perhaps the easiest role for the founder CTO to step into, as they have the historical context for the company and can most genuinely and passionately tell the company story and evangelize its product and value.

## Transitioning Between Types

Ideally, a startup CTO will prove adept in all three areas, though most people will specialize in just one or two. If your business needs a focus that isn't your expertise, it may be worth asking yourself if you can execute that task more effectively by delegating it to a coworker. Especially at an early stage startup, most technical cofounder/cofounder CTOs will be internal tech-focused. Usually there's not much other work to be done at this stage!

It's a very common pattern for that person to find themselves stretching into internal people or external focuses as the company grows, and that's not always a desirable transition for that person. It's not a personal failure to admit that your specialty or your motivation is in tech and that people management isn't a great fit, but quite the opposite. Identifying your superpowers and architecting a role in the company to leverage that superpower is how you add the most value, and the company should hire somebody else whose superpower is, for example, people management to fill that role.

If you find yourself stuck in a role you're unhappy with, it's vital that you acknowledge the mismatch both to yourself and to your CEO. This doesn't mean giving up your position as a founder or leader, or as a respected and high-impact person within the company.

Some thoughts on various transitions:

- Your Superpower: Internal Tech
  - Company Needs
    - Internal People.
      - Hire a people-focused VP of Engineering, proactively characterizing the role of CTO as technical.
    - External Focus
      - If you don't already have somebody in-house who is doing this better than you, then hire a developer evangelist and empower them to fulfill the role. Otherwise, promote from within and ensure it's clear what the role entails.

- Your Superpower: Internal People
  - Company Needs
    - Internal Tech
      - If you have a senior engineer or architect on the team whom you can empower/elevate to a position of technical leadership, that's worth considering. Otherwise, a technical architect should be near the top of your hiring priorities.
    - External Focus
      - If you don't already have somebody in-house who is doing this better than you, then hire a developer evangelist and empower them to fulfill the role. Otherwise, promote from within and ensure it's clear what the role entails.

- Your Superpower: External Focus
  - Company Needs
    - Internal Tech
      - If you have a senior engineer or architect on the team who you can empower/elevate to a position of technical leadership, that's worth considering. Otherwise, a technical architect should be near the top of your hiring priorities.
    - Internal People
      - Hire a people-focused VP of Engineering.

In many cases, the end outcome may mean hiring a CTO whose superpower is better aligned with what the company needs at the time. In other cases, it might mean hiring a very capable people-focused VP of Engineering to complement a highly technical CTO.

# 2

## TECHNICAL TEAM MANAGEMENT

Your output as a technical leader is measured by the output of your team, so it falls on you to ensure the team as a whole is running well. What "running well" means will vary by team and circumstance, but there are general patterns and trends that correlate with high performance. In this section, my goal is to provide guidance on situations common to all tech leaders.

## 2.1 Tech Culture and General Philosophy

I encourage all leaders to adopt the general leadership style known as *servant leadership*. As a servant leader your main focus is on serving the needs of your team. This means focusing on empowering others, building a culture of transparency, communication, collaboration, and growth. As you think about your team and culture, and about decisions on a day-to-day basis, ask yourself which option enables the team to do their best work and thus deliver the most for the business.

## TEN PILLARS OF TECH CULTURE

### 1. SPEND TEAM TIME ON THINGS THAT MATTER TO THE BUSINESS

In general, you want your team to be spending time on things that move the needle for the business, and it's your responsibility as technical leader to create an environment where your engineers can focus their efforts in this way with consistency and minimal distractions. This frame may seem obvious, but when used properly, it's a powerful tool for decision-making.

For example, say your team is debating between using an off-the-shelf framework for the backend vs. writing something from scratch. There's a nuanced list of pros and cons one could make that would discuss things like added flexibility from building from scratch vs. shorter time to first deployment with the framework. In this hypothetical reality, what your business really needs is to iterate on the frontend and optimize the customer journey, so every moment spent on the backend is one moment less spent moving the frontend forward. If the out-of-the-box solution is good enough to power that frontend iteration, even if you have to throw away the framework and rewrite the backend in eighteen months with a custom solution, iterating quickly on the frontend now and finding product market fit earns your business the right to do that rewrite down the line.

### 2. USE RELIABLE TOOLS WHERE YOU CAN AND INNOVATE WHERE IT COUNTS

Also referred to as "don't reinvent the wheel," and "standing on the shoulders of giants," the idea here is to use off-the-shelf components (libraries, cloud services, applications, packages) whenever possible. There's an inherent tradeoff for using off-the-shelf components between ease of getting started and customizing a solution to match your exact problem. I contend that in most circumstances where a pre-existing implementation already exists, the tradeoff leans heavily towards using the off-the-shelf service, library, or application.

In the rare circumstance where you will ultimately need to rewrite or heavily customize the dependency, the experience you had with the off-the-shelf tool will be very valuable in influencing and speeding up the design of the custom build.

## 3. AUTOMATION UNLOCKS VELOCITY

Your goal as the architect of your team is to ensure that your team spends as much of its time working on code that produces value for the business as possible. There are a number of time-consuming tasks developers do on a regular basis that are necessary to writing code but don't themselves add business value (e.g., replicating production environments, getting code to run locally, figuring out how to run test suites, provisioning feature branch environments in the cloud, tracking down bugs that aren't covered by tests, etc.).

These types of tasks impose a constant tax on overall productivity. You can avoid paying the tax by making an investment in automating these tasks whenever they are identified. Encourage your team to document whenever they are spending more than thirty minutes on nonproductive technical work and provide a space in your process for automating those tasks so nobody loses that hour ever again.

## 4. FREQUENCY REDUCES DIFFICULTY

Under the heading of "Frequency Reduces Difficulty," Martin Fowler expounds on the phrase, "If it hurts, do it more often" (ctohb.com/fowler). Any process or task that is painful, error-prone, or otherwise costly for your team, Fowler contends, is a symptom of that task being underdeveloped. Without pressure from you, painful technical tasks tend to be the last ones volunteered for. As a result, they're neglected, and the pain gets worse over time. Alternatively, if your team culture emphasizes prioritizing these painful tasks, then more effort will go into automating, documenting, and improving those tasks, making them ultimately less painful or even entirely automated. As Fowler points out, doing tasks more frequently also provides more feedback on them and builds skill with practice, all of which further reduce the difficulty and pain of the task.

For many teams, releasing code to production is an example of a task that is often painful. Releasing code can require hours of time to actually deploy and so it's done infrequently. If, however, your team subscribes to the "If it hurts, do it more often" philosophy, then you as the technical leader will push for regular releases at faster intervals. If you start with a weekly release, then the first week the team will feel the pain, and the second week will be just as painful as the first, but perhaps the engineers will notice an opportunity to automate a piece of the deployment. By the third, fourth, or fifth release, you'll likely have an entirely new set of scripts and infrastructure to get code out the door, enabling you to accelerate the release frequency to twice a week. After a while, you'll be able to get code out the door with the push of a button. Releasing more than once per day is referred to as Continuous Deployment (see Continuous Deployment, page 216).

## 5. STANDARDIZE THE RFC PROCESS

An RFC, or Request for Comment, is a document that outlines a technical idea, process, or specification and is written for the purpose of peer review and subsequent adoption. Most protocols you're familiar with have an associated RFC, such as RFC 2616 for HTTP, or RFC 1035 for DNS. The idea of peer review and subsequent adoption and standardization is a powerful tool for pseudo-democratically making technical decisions and getting buy-in on the results, and it can be a great tool to use with your team.

I recommend that you formalize an RFC process and provide some guidance as to what kinds of decisions should be put through the RFC process. A formal process can look like a simple checklist and a template document that includes where to put your copy of that document, how feedback/comments are collected, and what the process for voting, finalizing, and standardizing the document looks like.

My suggestion is to lean into the tools you have and, for example, create a markdown document in source control that acts as the RFC template. A new RFC would then be a pull request on that repository introducing a new markdown file with the proposal. It is then somewhat natural to collect "votes" as approvals on that pull request, and finalization of the RFC is when the pull request is ultimately merged. Alternatively, if you've set up an internal wiki, you can create an RFC there, and use a wiki's comment system to collect feedback.

You should also set clear expectations for what kinds of decisions get put to RFC. I recommend limiting it to high-level processes, technical opinions, and culture, and not using it for tool choice or system architecture. Some good examples of topics to RFC:

- Standardizing naming conventions (master vs. main, black/whitelist vs. allow/denylist, camelCase vs snake_case in various contexts)
- Usage of code formatters/static code analysis
- Meeting cadences/agenda/artifacts
- Monorepo vs. manyrepo
- API Design opinions/philosophies

I encourage you to include a section in your RFC template on how the results of an RFC are institutionalized. For example, if the RFC proposes standardizing a technical opinion for your team, once the RFC is ratified, that opinion should be incorporated into your engineering guidebook and onboarding documentation, so it becomes canon for current and future employees as well.

## 6. MAKE SPEED A GOAL, NOT A STRATEGY

In *Good Strategy/Bad Strategy,* author Richard Rumelt defines a good strategy as one that provides three elements: a diagnosis of how to overcome a challenge, a guiding policy or an overall approach, and a set of actions for how the policy is to be carried out. Strategy outlines the journey.

In contrast, a goal is a description of a destination. I've heard countless teams tell me their strategy is to go fast, with no outline of how they get there. I'm entirely in agreement that engineering velocity and speed is a great goal, but it's not a strategy.

Here's a sample strategy for delivering high-velocity engineering:

- **Challenge:** We're an unregulated, early stage startup that needs to iterate as fast as possible to find product market fit before we run out of capital.

- **Diagnosis:** We have an opportunity to minimize complexity and move quickly. Since we don't yet have product market fit, the value of what we've built so far is minimal, so we need to ignore sunk cost and opt for fast rewrites while we're still unsure what our product will look like long term.

- **Action plan:** We will focus on hiring software engineering generalists, reinforce a culture of curiosity and scrappiness, leave ego at the door, and invest only a modest amount of effort into long-term technical planning. Instead, for now, we'll focus on our ability to ship MVP product experiments to the market.

## 7. PARTICIPATE IN CONTINUOUS EDUCATION AND TECHNOLOGY CONFERENCES

Technology conferences are ubiquitous nowadays, and there's a gathering of like-minded individuals for nearly every subspeciality of software engineering. Your team, if they haven't already, will likely ask at some point for a budget to attend these conferences. A typical budget request would be for $1,000 for air and hotel, and $500–$1,000 for entry fees and per-diem expenses. All in all, it will cost on the order of $2,000 for an engineer to attend a conference, plus their time out of the office. Both in the spirit of learning and continuous improvement, as well as a host of ancillary benefits, I recommend that you budget for and regularly approve or systematically approve conference requests.

If the only benefit of attending a conference were that the employee learned a bit more about a relevant technical topic that they're passionate about, the cost would be worth it. There are, however, many more benefits. I encourage you to require conference attendees to produce a written document summarizing key things they learned after they return. You should also consider sponsoring the conferences most relevant to your business and having you or one of your team members host a seminar on a particular topic. These seminars and sponsorships provide excellent branding opportunities for your company, getting your name and message in front of a very targeted audience—an audience that likely contains candidates you'd like to hire in the future.

In summary, allocating a budget for engineers to attend conferences is good for individual professional development, with a fairly low-effort documentation exercise. This can be good for team learnings and is a great opportunity through networking, sponsorship, or hosting to recruit future members of the team.

## 8. DEPLOY RUBBER DUCK DEBUGGING

Have you ever had the experience of trying to work through a problem and, while explaining it to a coworker, figured out the solution? Rubber Duck Debugging (ctohb.com/rdd, ctohb.com/tpp) is a simple practice that attempts to replicate this phenomenon without involving or context-switching a coworker.

Rubber Duck Debugging is the process of working through a problem by first speaking the problem out loud, perhaps at a real physical rubber duck that is sitting on your desk. The idea is that by speaking the problem out loud, often one will hear the flaw, or see a solution to the problem, that they hadn't considered when the problem was only in their head. The "rubber duck" approach potentially saves a coworker an interruption and gets you an answer faster.

## 9. BUILD AN EXPLAINER VIDEO LIBRARY

If a picture is worth a thousand words, a one-minute video of your desktop/IDE/application with your voice discussing a technical topic is worth $1,000 in developer time savings. There are many tools that make it trivially easy to record and share these mini video messages, including tools built into Slack and Loom. Not only can you clearly convey a technical idea more easily with a screen recording and voiceover than text, but you can do it on your own time. The resulting video can be sped up at the viewer's discretion, and the video can be archived and rewatched later as part of an organizational knowledge base.

As the technical leader of your team, I encourage you to regularly make these mini video explainers, especially at times when you're making changes to the architecture of the platform. Organize all the videos in a library in your internal wiki. Make sure they're complete and standalone but short and to the point; if you don't get around to critical content until the end of an overlong video, your team members might never see it. Also, make the approach as consistent as possible so viewers know what to expect.

I guarantee you'll get relatively poor watch rates upfront as you make and distribute the videos, but over time that library will provide tremendous value as a source of reference knowledge and will get views that save you and your team meaningful amounts of time.

## 10. ONBOARDING IS EVERYBODY'S RESPONSIBILITY

Your team is continuously creating tribal knowledge, be it how to start a service, or how code patterns are used across your codebase. There are two ways to deal with this: you can do nothing, and on a daily basis you'll increase the size of the knowledge gap for new employees, or you can actively work on converting siloed tribal knowledge into scalable documentation for current and future employees. For obvious reasons, I recommend the latter. This means everyone should always be asking themselves, "How can I document what I've just created/learned/discovered?" And when you have new employees who come across something that they can't find in your knowledge base, it's up to them to seek out an answer and document it.

# 2.2 Tech Debt

San Francisco's Golden Gate Bridge is made out of steel, which is not actually golden in color. The bridge is painted, and maintaining the iconic color of the bridge is so important to San Franciscans that they paint it continuously (ctohb.com/painting). Once repainting is finished, the process immediately restarts. This form of continuous investment or perpetual maintenance is what's required to keep the most important and sophisticated systems performing to expectations, from the Golden Gate Bridge to your team's software project. Only for your project, the maintenance doesn't require paint buckets; it comes in the form of technical debt.

Every feature a software development team delivers brings with it some level of need for future work, or debt. That debt can take the form of bugs that need fixing, fast-follows to the feature to deliver incremental customer value, or sloppiness in the code that should be fixed to improve maintainability, performance, or security. A certain amount of debt naturally accrues even if your team is out on vacation: security vulnerabilities in dependent software are found, packages go out of date, new versions of tools are released, third-party APIs are deprecated or changed, etc. Debt is unavoidable and you need to account for it.

## TECH DEBT AND THE PRODUCT LIFECYCLE

Another way to think of tech debt is like financial debt, such as a mortgage on a house. When you take out a mortgage to buy a house, you're making a deliberate decision to take on debt, knowing the consequences (interest), to enable you to do something you want now (get a house). Then you pay down that debt on a consistent basis over an extended period of time (monthly payments).

The same happens with technology debt. Your startup may accumulate it deliberately as part of a conscious tradeoff, and part of that tradeoff is establishing a realistic plan for paying it down. You should apply the same kind of logic you would to pay down financial debt to addressing your technical debt: either pay it off upfront because you have extra resources (and no better place to put those resources), pay it off continuously over time, or pay it all off down the road but perhaps at a higher total price that includes interest.

However you choose to pay down your tech debt, the key to doing so successfully is to recognize that debt is an inevitable part of the software engineering process, and proactively paying down debt is a necessary investment in overall engineering health.

### DEFINING TECH DEBT

Another way to define technical debt is as a technical decision, implementation, or nuance that actively reduces the efficiency or effectiveness of the business today or in the future. The point is that tech debt has a consequence that matters. Some of your code might be objectively ugly or inefficient, but if that inefficiency has no impact on the business and there's no need to modify that code in the future to maintain quality, performance, or iteration, then that code isn't costly in terms of tech debt. After all, the goal of software development, especially at a startup, is not to write the perfect codebase, but to build software that enables the business.

Don't be afraid of debt. It can serve a purpose. For example, when building Version 1 of a product that's not yet been validated in the market, a technical team may decide on an architecture that will not scale past a hundred users. If that decision allows the team to rapidly validate the product and determine whether or not a hundred users will ever use the product, that path may be worthwhile especially given the fact that it may take several versions of these prototypes to find one that users love.

There are at least seven types of technical debt:

- **Architecture** or **Design Debt** arises when the design of the software is not capable of meeting the near-term or future needs of the business. For example, the design makes it too challenging to build the features the business needs, or the design won't scale to the number of users or performance requirements of the business.

- **Code Debt** accrues when the implementation itself was done without paying attention to best practices, yielding code that's difficult to understand and maintain.

- **Test Debt** accumulates when you've run insufficient automated tests to provide the team confidence in the correctness of the codebase.

- **Infrastructure Debt** occurs when the infrastructure, observability, and supporting systems are not robust or have been poorly maintained, leading to difficulty scaling or deploying updates, or poor uptime and reliability.

- **Documentation Debt** results when there's insufficient documentation, or the documentation is stale/inaccurate, which can make it difficult for team members to onboard a project.

- **Skill Debt** rises when the team members lack the needed skills to maintain or update the code or surrounding infrastructure.

- **Process Debt** accrues when the team is inconsistent in how it solves problems, leading to mistakes, delays, or increased costs.

## TECH DEBT BANKRUPTCY

If your startup neglects or ignores tech debt for long enough, it can become a major impediment to future progress. Teams can unintentionally find themselves spending 80 or even 100 percent of their time sorting through system problems or inefficiencies as a result of tech debt, a state known as "tech debt bankruptcy."

Some signs your team may be tech debt-bankrupt:

- You are regularly dealing with production outages to the point of material business impact.

- You receive constant pushback or exaggerated timelines on new features due to the need to deal with debt.

- The team complains that a codebase is too complex to get work done.

- New features cannot be shipped without accidentally breaking old features or introducing an unacceptably high level of defects.

If you find yourself in tech debt bankruptcy, it's time to raise the alarm, reset expectations with stakeholders, devise a plan to consolidate the debt, and begin paying it down immediately.

If you've been honest with your peers in leadership (see Delivering Bad News, page 46), you should have the necessary credibility to explain the tech debt problem and develop a common understanding of the ROI for an investment in resolving tech debt.

## MEASURING DEBT—THE DEBT INVENTORY

Unlike with a mortgage or car loan, there's no website you can visit that will give you a statement of your exact amount of tech debt and remaining payments. Some forms of debt can be measured quantitatively, but most of the analysis is qualitative. For healthy and responsible debt management at scale, I recommend a debt inventory survey.

The survey should be taken at regular intervals. Somewhere from one to four times per year, do a sober analysis across the varying kinds of debt, producing an honest assessment of where the team is operating. Don't take the survey independently; rather, do so in collaboration with other engineers on the team who are working in the code every day and interacting with the debt on a regular basis.

A survey can be as simple as this: for each of the following types of debt, rate how much we have on a scale of 1 to 10, then provide a few sentences justifying the score.

Use the results of the survey to inform how your team spends its energy paying down debt, and compare results between surveys over time to ensure debt stays at a reasonable level and your team is regularly solving its biggest debt pain points.

## STRATEGIES FOR PAYING DOWN DEBT

In order to decide when to pay down tech debt, you should first consider how much of your team's time is worth spending on it. Key considerations include:

- How much debt exists, as indicated by your most recent debt inventory survey

- How much it is hindering your company's ability to run day to day—i.e., via outages, customer churn, or defect rates

- How much it is hurting your team's ability to deliver on new projects

- How difficult it will be to pay down the debt

If you are not in tech debt bankruptcy and your goal is to maintain a healthy level of debt, I recommend allocating somewhere between 10–20 percent of your team's time to investments in non-feature engineering (e.g., paying down debt, exploring new patterns/proofs of concept, improving developer experience, etc.). The more severe your current debt impact, and the higher the effort to pay down the debt, the higher the percentage of your team's time you should allocate.

### JUST-IN-TIME PAYMENT

The most common way to handle tech debt is to pay it off on a "Just-in-Time" basis, meaning the debt is paid off as part of a business-driven project. This will often look like a team adding tech debt tickets that relate to the stories that have been selected for a sprint in a planning meeting. This is a low-overhead and low-planning-effort approach, and it can work out well. But be mindful of some potential pitfalls:

- Just-in-time payments, by virtue of being less visible to the broader team, can lead to systemic underinvestment in tech debt. Make sure you are being honest and transparent with the team as you do just-in-time-payment about what total percentage of team time you're expecting to be in debt.

- Adding tech debt as part of a sprint can imply that investing in tech debt is a secondary objective to the sprint goals, and thus likely to get cut from scope if a team runs low on time.

- Tackling tech debt in a sprint may be perceived as slowing down the sprint or causing delays, rather than as an investment in velocity and overall system health.

## PERIODIC PAYDOWN

Periodic paydown is akin to how one might pay down a car loan or a mortgage. The team makes space to pay off debt on a fixed interval (e.g., a day per sprint, a couple of days per month, or a couple of weeks per quarter). Google famously allowed their engineers "20 percent time" to work on whatever they wanted, including paying down debt or innovating on new projects and tools. The idea here is the same: as a manager, you explicitly make time and encourage the team to make investments into the tools and processes used to do engineering.

For example, the "Shape Up" method (see Tech Process, page 157) describes a two-week cooldown period after a six-week cycle, or 25 percent of an eight-week period, for making technical investments. Keep in mind that 25 percent isn't a magic number; the right percentage will depend on your team's debt inventory.

## CONTINUOUS PAYDOWN

Depending on how expensive debt is for your team, you may want to dedicate more resources to overall system quality than a periodic strategy allows. This looks like having a dedicated team—what I call a customer crew in a two-crew scenario (see Project Maintenance: "The 'Two Crews' Philosophy," page 113)—pay down tech debt as part of their everyday work and objectives.

It's important to ensure that any team whose primary objective is internal efficiency, such as a tech debt team or a customer crew, has clear and measurable goals for their work. For example, if your debt inventory ranks test debt as your highest debt category, then measure defect rates and code coverage and hold the customer crew accountable for improving those metrics. If your infrastructure debt is the largest, then focus on uptime and Mean Time to Recovery metrics.

## COMMUNICATION OF TECH DEBT

Non-technical leaders don't expect perfection from their technical teams. But they do expect high performance and consistently met expectations.

When it comes to debt, that means clearly communicating your strategy for keeping debt at a manageable level, and also providing upfront and honest communication about when debt may get in the way of business goals, as well as your strategy for paying it down so it's no longer a blocker.

# 2.3 Technology Roadmap

## TIMEFRAMES

I find it useful to think of a technology roadmap in three timeframes, sometimes labeled as "short-, medium-, and long-term" or "horizon one, two, and three." Each timeframe should be managed by a different process and is often owned by different stakeholders.

|  | Short-Term/Horizon One | Medium-Term/Horizon Two | Long-Term/Horizon Three |
|---|---|---|---|
| Owner | Tech leads | Middle management (directors) | Senior management (CTO, VPE) |
| Calendar Time Frame | 2–3 weeks | 1–3 months | 1–3 years |
| Management Process/Artifacts | Day-to-day process (e.g., Sprints, Kanban, Tickets) | Team roadmap (spreadsheet or project management software) | Quarterly/yearly goals, OKRs, strategic vision documents |
| Example Subject Matter/Scope | Individual features or items of tech debt | Feature groups/business initiatives, architectural projects, incremental cost optimization | Replatforming, team growth/organization, programming language transitions, architectural rewrites |

## SHORT-TERM/HORIZON ONE

Your short-term roadmap is what your team is working on now. This includes any in-flight features, actively worked-on defects, tech debt, or urgent work items. For more detail on managing your short-term roadmap, see "Workflow" in the Tech Process section, page 157.

## MEDIUM-TERM/HORIZON TWO

If you're the only technical manager on the team, then you are responsible for both the medium- and long-term roadmaps. If you have directors or senior managers reporting to you, you'll likely be collaborating on the medium-term roadmap. The medium-term roadmap is a very useful artifact not only for your own planning and organization but also as a tool to communicate with other departments/stakeholders on what the engineering team is doing.

Typically, a medium-term roadmap is implemented as a spreadsheet where teams or individuals are rows, and columns are time periods—often weeks or sprints—and the contents of the table are high-level work items or work areas. The purpose of the roadmap is not to predict precisely when any given task will be completed; doing so would require accurate and precise estimates of work which is tenuous at best (even at a granularity of weeks) and never a guarantee. Instead, the idea is to outline an order of operations and set a direction for the team.

You can and should expect to update the actual duration of any given activity as engineering progresses. Updating the number of weeks on a given task is a great point in time to evaluate whether continued investment in a project makes sense, and also to update external stakeholders on current completion estimates. Finally, the roadmap is helpful as a retrospective tool for tracking how long major initiatives took, and also to assess where a team is investing time at a very high level.

## LONG-TERM/HORIZON THREE

As the leader of your team, it falls on you to focus on the long-term health and productivity of the team. You should spend time designing these goals and producing a well-thought-out, clear document (or slide deck, video, wiki article, etc.) that explains the goals to the team. Once you've set initial goals, revisit them infrequently as changing strategic goals causes churn in an organization. Just as problematically, frequent changes in direction can be confusing and demotivating for the team. I encourage you to provide an update on progress towards long-term initiatives on a quarterly basis, both to the entire engineering team as well as to other executive leaders.

Some examples of long-term initiatives:

- Architectural tech debt
  - Moving from a deprecated framework to something actively maintained
  - Migrating from one hosting environment to another (e.g., onboarding to Kubernetes)
- Language debt
  - Consolidating usage of programming languages
  - Moving from older to newer versions of languages (Python 2 to 3, or .NET 4 to .Net 5+)
- Platform/architecture adoption
  - Having multiple teams adopt or migrate to new versions of internal services
  - Moving to/from serverless environments
  - Adopting new paradigms (e.g., server-side rendering, edge computing)
- Hiring plans
  - Growing or reorganizing teams
  - Hiring specialists or building new technical departments

## TIMELINE COMMUNICATION

Every leader in sales, marketing, product, or support I've worked with has been appreciative of transparency in the technical process and technical roadmap. By contrast, I've spoken to leaders at some companies who describe their technical teams as a "black hole." It goes without saying that you don't want to be called a black hole. Not being a black hole is simple; it looks like somewhere in your organization having a regular process to provide transparency to other leaders. Ideally, you're also helping other departments feel heard by having a forum, or a mechanism, to take input and incorporate that into the roadmap process. You can also close the loop and your process communicates back to stakeholders where their request is in the development process and manages expectations for when it will be ready.

## 2.4 Tech Process

Conway's Law states that "Organizations, who design systems, are constrained to produce designs which are copies of the communication structures of these organizations." Said another way, how you structure your teams, and importantly the process of work within and between those teams, will have a significant impact on the product you make. Teams working in information silos are unlikely to produce products that beautifully integrate with another team's designs, so it's up to you, as the overseer and ultimate architect of these communication structures, to ensure those structures meet the needs of the product you're developing.

Technical work is a highly nuanced matter with thousands of minute decisions that will affect how things ultimately interoperate and behave. To have any hope of maintaining productivity within your organization you need a set of standards and guiding principles to ensure the everyday technical decisions are broadly consistent and thus manageable for the team. That means you need to actually set those standards, train the team on them and have a day-to-day process to enforce and modify them as necessary.

The pattern a team follows to determine how to decide what to build and how work gets done is referred to as a workflow. The five most popular workflow patterns are:

- Agile
- SCRUM
- Kanban

- Waterfall

- Shape Up

There are entire books written on these patterns, and my favorite is *Scrum: The Art of Doing Twice the Work in Half the Time* by Jeff Sutherland. There are some fundamental strengths and weaknesses of these approaches that I'll discuss in this chapter; however, in the real world, the differences between the processes are dwarfed by the impact of how well the manager implements the chosen process. Your job as tech leader is to pick a process and ensure it's implemented well and iterated on.

A good development process respects the following truisms about software development:

- Nobody can perfectly predict how long it will take to complete any given engineering task.

- Engineering is rarely a straight line; building feature X may require putting time into problem Y before X can be built.

- There is no such thing as a perfect specification; there are always gaps and things to be discovered along the way in building technology.

Generally, the goal of a workflow process is to ensure that a team is well organized and delivering at an acceptable pace. In a roundabout way, some workflow processes even attempt to quantify engineering team velocity, allowing for reporting on how velocity changes over time to non-technical stakeholders.

## WATERFALL

The oldest workflow process, dating back to the 1950s, is waterfall (see ctohb.com/waterfall). The waterfall model breaks down project activities into sequential steps, where each step is dependent on and starts after the prior step is completed. In software engineering that looks something like first having a product vision, then doing product concepting, then product design, then software development, and finally testing, deployment, and maintenance. The most common criticism of waterfall is that this structure is rigid, inflexible, and doesn't promote iterative development.

## AGILE/SCRUM

Agile and SCRUM process is a more nuanced and prescriptive methodology than waterfall. There are many great resources that cover these nuances in detail, including Sutherland's *Scrum, Agile Estimating and Planning* by Mike Cohn, *The Art of Agile Development* by James Shore & Shane Warders.

The key thing to realize about these processes is that they are guidelines, not scripture. To get the best out of your engineering team, start with a process and see how well it works for your particular group of people with your particular type of technical challenges. Some teams have work that lends itself much more to estimation and story pointing, while others have much more ambiguous brownfield projects where estimation is near impossible. Pay attention to whether any particular ceremony from the process is really adding value to the engineering team, or if it's just a lengthy meeting everyone dreads.

Do not hesitate to skip ceremonies that aren't obvious wins for the team. For example, I find SCRUM's prescription for planning poker to be inefficient for most teams.

## SHAPE UP

Shape Up is a methodology formalized by the company Basecamp and published in an eBook available at basecamp.com/shapeup. The core cycle in Shape Up is six weeks long, a much longer sprint than espoused by SCRUM. This cycle uses fixed-time and variable scoping. The idea is that a longer time period provides more space to produce clear pitches (specifications) and do good work on a project. Shape Up places considerably less emphasis on estimation than other models—which, as I'll soon discuss, is a good thing for engineering teams.

## ENGINEERING ESTIMATES

According to Google, the technical definition of accuracy is "the degree to which the result of a measurement, calculation, or specification conforms to the correct value or a standard." That is to say, accuracy is an indicator of overall correctness. When you're throwing darts at a dartboard and aiming for the bullseye, an accurate set of throws is a set of throws that tends towards the center.

Precision, by contrast, is defined technically as "refinement in a measurement, calculation, or specification, especially as represented by the number of digits given." In other words, precision indicates a level of exactness. When throwing darts, if all of your throws, regardless of their target, are tightly grouped together, that can be said to be a precise grouping.

As this description should help you visualize, something can be accurate without being precise (a broad grouping of darts around or near the bullseye but not hitting it), precise without being accurate (a tight grouping of darts that misses the bullseye), and, of course, both accurate and precise (a tight grouping of darts that does hit the bullseye).

You should expect—and hold your team accountable for—accurate but not necessarily precise estimates for completing software development tasks. If today is the first of the month, reasonable guidance from your team is, "We'll ship the feature this month." If the team says, "We'll ship the feature on the 23rd," they're more likely to miss that deadline.

There's no need to try to estimate hours or days per ticket if you plan your work/resource allocation out by week, month, or quarter. Pay attention over time to whether or not your estimates are actually giving you the planning capability you hope for. If they're not, don't punish the team by continuing the process, or worse, using it as a contributing factor in performance reviews. Instead, adjust the estimates so they help instead of hurting you. Change your expectations, and instead of reacting to missing estimates, react to the challenges the team is facing as they struggle to meet the estimates.

A final note on estimates: don't conflate missing estimates with poor total output/velocity. Some teams will be highly effective, have high output, and still miss estimates. Velocity is the more important metric, and a high output but imperfectly estimating team should not be punished. Conversely, a team that regularly misses estimates *and* has trouble delivering new value is underperforming and needs to change.

## BURNDOWN CHARTS

SCRUM burndown charts show team progress against estimates and can be a great tool for measuring sprint productivity. However, estimates are imperfect and, for various reasons, a burndown chart may show a flat line or even burn up. This can be because a team legitimately is not making progress, or it could be an artifact of estimation issues or bad data collection.

A burndown chart that burns up consistently, despite teams shipping and doing good work, is demoralizing and not achieving the intended benefit. If there are easy adjustments that will help you better capture data and fix the chart, make that change. But if you find a particular way of measuring output still isn't working, just get rid of it. It's okay to admit that your method of estimating these particular types of stories with this team isn't precise enough and move on to other methods of monitoring and improving performance.

In my experience, only a small percentage of teams find success with burndown charts, so don't be disheartened if that one technique isn't helpful for your engineering team.

## CHOOSING A WORKFLOW

I contend that which workflow you choose will not be a significant factor in the ultimate success and velocity of your engineering team. The key factor is that you are paying attention to your team's workflow and continuously iterating on the workflow itself to ensure your patterns are adding value and are a good match, both for your team and the types of problems your team faces.

That said, here is a rough model for thinking about which type of workflow is likely to be a better starting place: well-understood work (i.e., tasks that are concrete, greenfield, and easy to explain) is easier to manage and will generate more benefit with a more nuanced or prescriptive planning process. Said another way, if your work is ambiguous and hard to estimate, it's likely better managed with Kanban than SCRUM.

Well-understood stories that tend to work well with SCRUM are:

- Greenfield—that is, new code that doesn't depend on perhaps legacy or difficult-to-work-with external modules

- Not dependent on new patterns/tools/technologies, relying instead on the existing ("boring") tech stack

- Easily broken down from stories to smaller tasks

- Familiar to the team from previous work

Conversely, you're perhaps better with Kanban if your work is:

- Brownfield, or heavily impeded by tech debt with unclear paths for paydown/refactoring

- Regularly changing or saddled with unpredictable priorities

- Dependent on adopting new and different tools and patterns that can introduce unexpected costs in the first few implementations

- Assigned to a brand-new team that doesn't have a history working together or on these types of projects

## COOLDOWN/INNOVATION SPRINTS

When using a regular cadence like sprints, the major peril teams find themselves in is the expectation that a sprint will finish, features will be shipped, and the team can immediately shift to the next set of features. Due to the accumulation of debt and need to iterate on product features, that is simply not possible to sustain. There has to be either continuous or periodic time set aside to pay for debt.

A common practice for periodically paying down debt is the notion of a "cooldown" sprint. Sometimes called a "tech debt" sprint, or "innovation sprint," the idea is the same: give the team time to clean up their digital workspace, do some code-housekeeping and ensure that they and the code are in a good place for high velocity work going forward. As discussed in Strategies for Paying Down Debt, page 150, it's reasonable to dedicate anywhere from 5-20 percent of your total development time on cooldown work. If you're doing two-week sprints, that might mean that one in four or five sprints is dedicated to cooldown.

## TECHNICAL PLANNING AND SPECIFICATIONS

When discussing the process for writing tech specs with engineers, I'm often asked, "How do you have time to write specs?" Usually I counter with, "How do you have time *not* to write tech specs?" Implied in my response is that taking time to think through what you're building before you build it is a net time saver.

Software engineering is inherently a creative process, meaning we're not doing the same thing every time and there is more than one way to do any particular story. A great planning process recognizes that there is value to be gained in thinking through a story in advance but balances that emphasis on pre-planning with the knowledge that the only real way to truly know everything about a feature is to actually build it.

A great tech planning process can accomplish several goals:

- Reduce the amount of rework in a feature

- Identify ways to do less work to achieve the same functionality

- Decrease the chance that important non-business visible considerations are forgotten, such as error handling/negative cases, testing, logging, monitoring, analytics, security, scalability, launch planning, and tech debt payoff

- Increase the chance that work from multiple people/teams is done in a compatible way

- Provide valuable documentation for how and why a feature was built a certain way for future maintenance, improvement, or expansion

- Keep the team thoughtful and aligned on irreversible/expensive technical considerations (e.g., tooling and architecture), as well as unlikely-to-forget key details

- Prove lightweight enough that it is completable in reasonable time and doesn't force decisions on minor details that either don't matter or don't have enough information upfront

## TECH SPEC LEADS

I recommend that you designate a lead for any project that needs planning: a single person to be accountable for producing the technical specification and getting that specification through your approval workflow. That doesn't mean they're the only contributor. On the contrary, if other team members are available during the planning window and have helpful knowledge, they can and should contribute.

Planning can be synchronous (i.e., everyone is in a room for the whole time period) or asynchronous. I recommend asynchronous planning as much of the work in planning will involve research (e.g., reading product documentation, reading code, prototyping/proof of concepting, evaluating tools and APIs, etc.) which can be done fine independently.

## TIME FOR PLANNING

Your tech planning process should save you time in your initial implementation. It should also save time in the future by minimizing tech debt and leaving behind documentation that can accelerate future improvements. The wrong amount of time to put into planning doesn't meet these goals, either because it's too short and doesn't save you time/produce good documentation, or is so lengthy that it doesn't pay for itself in savings.

There is no universal formula for the correct amount of time, but I'll provide a rule of thumb: allocate one day to technical planning for every week of work you estimate the project to take. In general, this will lead to between half-day and three-day planning windows. If your project requires less than two days of work, it likely needs very minimal planning effort and has low risk. Conversely, if you're looking at a project that is expected to take more than three solid weeks of development effort, you may not be able to efficiently plan something that large all at once and should consider breaking it down.

If your team refuses to invest time into planning, you're likely pushing too hard for results over process. The way to ensure the engineering process produces good results for the business is not to crack the whip harder, but to establish a healthy process that enables good results. You wouldn't speed up a structural engineering team designing a bridge by having them work longer hours. You would make sure they have the best bridge-designing tools available to them with the best possible information about the span being bridged. Software engineering is no different. But instead of using CAD software or real-world measurements of soil/rock, we have product specifications, design process, and software tools.

Conversely, an overly lengthy planning process where team members insist on getting every minute detail upfront can be an indicator of a serious cultural problem, where team members are paralyzed by fear of making a mistake. Effective planning won't eliminate risk, but thinking through important, high-level decisions in advance can minimize it. A team that obsesses over details may be afraid of making mistakes or unwilling to iterate on their work—both symptoms of overly results-driven management. Individuals should not be punished for reasonable mistakes or planning oversights. It's fine if a tech spec isn't perfect upfront; expect your team to find mistakes or gaps during implementation, and update the spec when those issues are found.

## Prototyping as Part of Spec Writing

Often when writing a technical specification you'll have multiple options for how to achieve a goal without any overtly compelling arguments on paper to go one way or another. Or you'll discover unknowns about the effectiveness of a particular option, which makes the decision ambiguous. If possible—especially if it can be done efficiently—I encourage you to give your engineering teams space to prototype one or more of these solutions to gain data to make better decisions in planning. Half a day devoted to building a toy with a new tool to validate that the tool will achieve the desired results upfront is half a day well spent.

## TECH SPEC CONTENT

Having a template that your team uses when starting to write a technical specification is a great way to speed things up and ensure important topics aren't neglected. I recommend your template primarily be a sequence of headings with topic areas to be covered, perhaps with a bit of instruction or reminder for tech spec authors. I've included a sample tech spec at ctohb.com/templates.

A quick aside before jumping into content: technical documents can be a bit dry and serious. If it aligns with your culture, I encourage you to inject lightheartedness where it's appropriate and not distracting. A good example is a clever meme at the top of the document that references the subject of the specification. In my experience, it takes only a manager/leader making a meme once in a spec to encourage others on the team (read: open the floodgates) to add their own.

Some suggested components to include in the template:

- A reminder that the document is in fact a template, and authors should make a copy before starting writing (this mistake is easy to make!)

- Guidance for how a specification should be thought about/a reference to company specification guidelines and approval processes

- A background section explaining the business rationale for the project

- Any particularly standout areas of technical risk this project has (e.g., it touches sensitive PII, or involves previously unused tools/architecture)

- A glossary/definition of any non-obvious terms

- Any explicit business goals the spec aims to achieve/correlation with previously stated goals (i.e., quarterly KPIs or OKRs)

- A solution architecture overview (the bulk of the document)

- Tech debt—specifically discuss why or why not addressing any required/adjacent debt

- Data modeling, including required updates to a database or data pipelines

- Internal and external reporting or analytics and measurement requirements

- Testing

- Deployment

- Feature toggles/flags

- Implications on overall system reliability or disaster recovery

- Security and privacy

- Deliverable milestones

## TECH SPEC APPROVAL

To achieve the goal of ensuring consistency and alignment across projects and between team members, you must ensure team members are reading and contributing to each other's planning process. My recommendation to achieve this is to have a lightweight approval process for a specification before it can be considered complete.

## REVIEW GOALS

Your tech spec review goals should include the following:

- Ensure all teams/projects are aligned on technical direction and building consistently.

- Review and educate the team on important data concepts/technical contracts.

- Ensure universal and consistent understanding of the problem at hand.

- Minimize chance of missing important edge cases or other non-business visible requirements.

## REVIEW PROCESS

My recommendation for a lightweight review process is an asynchronous conversation in the document followed by a synchronous conflict resolution meeting (see Meetings and Time Management, page 28, for more on conflict resolution meetings). The author of the technical specification should, once they've made some progress on the key elements of the project, circulate the document with other engineers who have sufficient context. The idea is for others to read the document and leave comments and questions in their own time. Many of these issues can be resolved quickly and asynchronously by the lead author, but some may be contentious or highly nuanced, requiring higher bandwidth communication.

To close out the process, the author should schedule a meeting whose attendees are only those who have read the document and contributed in advance. The purpose of the meeting is to review open questions and conflicts and come to a resolution. The purpose of the meeting is not for the author to simply read the specification out loud to a bored or disinterested audience. If there are open questions that require further diligence to learn about and resolve, then do that offline and review the results with only the interested parties afterward.

Once all open questions are resolved, document who contributed to the specification (so a future reader knows to whom they should direct further questions), and consider the document approved.


## LEADERS IN SPECIFICATION REVIEW MEETINGS

The technical leader or manager does not have to be the approver for all technical documents. I encourage you to build a culture where the team as a whole feels safe to contribute and doesn't rely on you to provide technical guardrails or support. Early on, when the department is relatively small, you should be heavily involved in most or all specifications, but that approach won't scale. As soon as you've hired other senior individual contributors, architects, or managers, empower them to be lead reviewers and defer to them, allowing them to do the job you hired them for. If you find a senior member is not guiding the team well in these reviews, don't walk all over them in a public forum. Discuss and course-correct with them in private.

## TECHNICAL SPECIFICATIONS AS DOCUMENTATION

Your tech team is now spending time creating thoughtful documents that cover how you're engineering your product, and the team should be making fewer mistakes as a result. The last way that technical specifications help you is by providing useful resources for future engineers who need to augment or modify the work that's been done. I recommend that you create a well-organized and searchable directory (e.g., an internal wiki such as Confluence or Notion, or document storage like Google Drive), and that your team be diligent about ensuring all specification documents are added to the directory. It may also be helpful to link or refer to the specification in code comments to explain why something is implemented the way it is.

# 2.5 Developer Experience (DX)

DevOps tooling company Harness (harness.io) defines Developer Experience (DX) as "the overall interactions and feelings that the developer feels when working towards a goal. It is similar to the definition of User Experience (UX), except in this case the primary user is a software engineer."

Developer experience may not always be measured on a dashboard, but when it's designed poorly, the team knows it, and they may complain loudly about it. Bad developer experience can derail an engineer an entire afternoon—for example, an attempt to boot up the microservice to test it throws a cryptic traceback and the maintainer of the service is on vacation, so a mid-level engineer spins their wheels for hours just trying to get to a reliable build-execute-test loop.

Multiply this inefficiency by all the engineers on your team and all the various types of repositories, services, and projects that exist at your company and it can quickly spiral into losing person-months of productivity in direct time. Add in additional context-switching time spent bringing in others to help solve the problems, and poor DX quickly goes to the top of the list of areas that, when left unaddressed, can tank an otherwise high-performing engineering team.

There are two prerequisites to a great developer experience:

1. Tools that make it easy to have highly reliable and reproducible environments and dependency chains

2. Documentation and consistency in practices for how things are done

Thankfully, nowadays, many readily available tools and ecosystems can help with #1. Most programming languages have an ecosystem with standardized tools for dependency management and reproducible environments. It's up to you to identify and use them (e.g., npm, pipfile, etc.). Many of these systems produce a file called a "lock file."

The lock file is not for concurrency management to avoid deadlocks; it's designed to lock in place a specific instance of the dependency graph. You should be committing these lock files and making sure other developers and any build systems use them. The lock file helps guarantee that everyone on the team has installed an identical set of dependencies. If your chosen programming language does not provide those tools, then it's up to you to build that reproducibility—perhaps by using docker containers, makefiles, or the like.

Often the difference between good DX and bad DX is twenty or thirty minutes of upfront effort from somebody familiar with the codebase. It doesn't take long to ensure that basic build commands work in a fresh install, and that those commands are documented in a local README.

One opportunity for you as CTO to make this easier is to ensure that the build commands used across repositories and codebases at your company are consistent. Maybe it's always "docker compose up" or always "yarn run." Whatever it is, any developer should be able to "git clone" any repository, and then the first command that comes to mind to build and run the software works.

## PRIORITIZING DEVELOPER EXPERIENCE

Anything not on the product roadmap can be difficult to prioritize. Thankfully, DX rarely requires a large enough investment of time that it needs triaging on the roadmap. In the early days of your company, I prefer to follow the "Boy Scout Rule"—leave the codebase (or developer experience) better than you found it. Any time a developer encounters a problem building, running, or testing something, it is their responsibility to fix, document, or otherwise ensure that whoever comes to that code next has an easier time of it.

As systems start to get larger it can become an increasingly sizeable chore to get everything running locally together to test functionality. At this point it may be worth investing in DX more formally on the roadmap, or even with dedicated headcount, to ensure that tools are working and developers don't lose large chunks of time fighting the system instead of writing productive code.

## EASY DEVELOPER EXPERIENCE WINS

Here are a few easy wins to upgrade DX across your software engineering team:

- Have a README file with instructions to run a codebase—ideally a one-liner to install dependencies—then build and run the code.

- Enforce that all code be linted with a strict set of linting rules that is consistent across all usages of that language at your company. Fail your builds if linting doesn't pass. If all developers have their IDE configured to auto-lint, builds should rarely fail for lint issues.

- Ensure that lint configuration is checked into source control where possible (i.e., by investing in setting up something like VSCode's settings.json file, found at ctohb.com/vscode).

- Invest time in making sure that local test data can be set up in local databases from scratch. Often a quick data generator or seed data script can short-circuit a lot of developer headaches. Better yet if the seed data can be easily augmented to add additional corner cases/use cases as the system evolves, so that the base set of test data can be as comprehensive/representative as possible.

- Develop a plan for how to either mock or actually spin up dependent services locally to test multiple-service interactions when necessary. Ideally, with good contracts and domain-driven design, the need for this will be rare, though it should still be easy when necessary.

## CHANGING TOOLS FOR DEVELOPER EXPERIENCE

In 2022, Stripe, the fintech decacorn (i.e., a company valued at more than $10 billion), decided that Flow, its current programming language, had become too expensive to use. It was using too much memory, locking up laptops, and integrated poorly with developer IDEs.

TypeScript, like Flow, is an optional type language built on top of JavaScript. TypeScript has seen far wider adoption than Flow, and thus has solved many of the problems the Stripe teams were encountering with Flow, which had become more painful to work with over time. It was increasingly clear that TypeScript offered a major DX improvement over Flow. The only problem is, how do you convert millions of lines of code from one language to another?

The answer, it turns out, is an eighteen-month project by a team of engineers to prepare for a single, massive merge commit to update the entire codebase all at once. On Sunday, March 6, 2022, Stripe's mega-merge landed, and on Monday, March 7, the team came back to work and started using a new programming language. One developer described the change as "the single biggest developer productivity boost in their time at Stripe."

The lesson here is that if the pain of poor developer experience is severe enough, then almost no cost is too high or any project out of reach to make improvements. Your team is almost certainly smaller than Stripe's, and you're likely not dealing with millions of lines of code, but the same calculus applies: if your team is encountering friction in DX that is slowing it down, you must invest the necessary developer time and effort to improve it to gain that efficiency back.

Another problem teams often face is changing tooling too often. In certain tech ecosystems (particularly the JavaScript world), it seems something new and shiny comes out every month that could provide a productivity boost for your team. I encourage you to be disciplined about adopting new tools, make sure you've spent the time to really understand the pain that exists, diligence the new tool, see if it meets *all* your requirements—not just the shiny headline—and make decisions accordingly. For more on my recommended process here, see Implementing Internal Technology Radar, page 204.

# 3

# TECH ARCHITECTURE

One of your key responsibilities as a tech leader is to make good decisions on your architecture and tools. Good architecture aligns the strengths of the tools and patterns you choose with the needs of your organization now and in the foreseeable future. That requires understanding the strengths, weaknesses, and tradeoffs inherent in each choice. My goal in this section of the book is to make you aware in general of the landscape of options in various domains, and help you recognize the general tradeoffs that different strategies entail.

One thing to keep in mind when discussing tools and tool choice with your team: engineers can be emotional about tool choice. Tools are reviewed as "good" and "bad," and people have personal likes, dislikes, and biases. As the leader and decision-maker, I strongly caution you against adopting this style of language when discussing tools. Not only can it potentially alienate team members if you're disparaging their personal favorite tool; it's also unproductive and can distract from the goal of identifying a good solution for your problem. Some individual tools are genuinely poorly designed and overshadowed by superior alternatives.

More often than not, a more nuanced evaluation will reveal that a given tool isn't inherently bad, but rather appropriate or inappropriate for a particular company or project. Don't let one bad past experience of trying to use a tool that was inappropriate for solving one problem prevent you or your team from using it another time when it may prove a better fit.

# 3.1 Architecture

There are many excellent resources that explore various architectural patterns deeply; one of my favorites is Martin Fowler's *Patterns of Enterprise Application Architecture.* In this chapter, I'll provide a summary of some key phrases you'll hear so you have context when exploring these topics in depth elsewhere.

## DOMAIN-DRIVEN DESIGN

Domain-driven design (DDD) is an approach to software development that focuses on understanding and modeling the problem domain in order to design better software solutions.

The core concepts of DDD include:

- **Domain model:** A representation of business concepts as objects in your technical system;

- **Ubiquitous language:** A common, consistent vocabulary and language that is used across your company to minimize confusion;

- **Bounded context:** The boundary within which the domain model applies and where the ubiquitous language is used.

## HIGH-LEVEL PATTERNS

When somebody uses the phrase "technical architecture," they are usually referring to how code is executed and how information moves around in a system. Most descriptions of architecture involve the phrases "services," "monoliths," or "message transports." This is in contrast to coding patterns, in which phrases such as "object-oriented," "functional programming," or "dependency injection" appear frequently. Coding patterns may sometimes be called "code architecture" and are discussed in Coding Patterns, page 188.

The highest-impact decision in technical architecture is whether code runs as a monolith or as a set of services (commonly referred to as microservices). I'll start here with a description of what each pattern looks like, and then provide some guidance on the tradeoffs between them.

### MONOLITHIC ARCHITECTURE

The monolithic architecture pattern is one in which all code is executed as a single process, where information moves between pieces of your system entirely in memory, modeled as simple function calls. If you've ever sat down and built a simple application in an afternoon, chances are good it would fall into the category of the monolith. Monoliths come in all sorts of shapes and sizes, from very small to massive, multi-million-line projects.

The key to building a successful monolith is to carefully design the data flows within the application, using domain-driven design. You can measure this pretty easily; you want to ensure that when a developer goes to change the functionality of the application, it is obvious where in the monolith they should be working. They should only need to change code in an obvious and well-defined or confined area to achieve their goal. Every additional "area" of the codebase that needs change to meet a functional requirement adds additional complexity or opportunity for error, and in general slows down development.

Key features of a monolith:

- Code is deployed as a single unit.

- Code is managed in a single source-code repository.

- Deployed code is scaled as a single unit up and down.

- Information moves between parts of the system in memory, usually with function calls.

- Domain-driven design and clear information flow design are not enforced by the system, leaving it up to the engineers to do design well.

## SERVICE-ORIENTED ARCHITECTURE (SOA)/MICROSERVICES

The phrase service-oriented architecture (SOA) originated in the 1990s and is used to refer to some fairly specific technology choices. Nowadays, the phrase is used to more broadly describe a system where information moves between parts of the system over a network. The main tradeoff with an SOA is that, in comparison to a monolith, it can be very complex to think about and requires a team to do a lot of setup and thoughtful design to truly ensure that the benefits outweigh added complexity.

Microservices are a subset of service-oriented architecture where each service is—as the name suggests—very small. There are system implementations with thousands of microservices, each of them only a few lines of code. That said, you do not need to have thousands of microservices to experience the benefits of a service-oriented architecture. Even breaking out a system into four or five smaller services, in the right circumstances, can provide major improvement to code health.

You may have heard that microservices are the only good architecture pattern; this is untrue. The perception stems from the fact that many monoliths are poorly designed or haven't received the attention and investment in tech debt required to unlock productivity. The idea that all microservice architectures are a joy to work in is also untrue. There are many microservice implementations that for one reason or another fail to realize the benefits as well.

Key features of an SOA or microservices system:

- Different services are independently deployable and scalable.

- Code is managed by either a single source-code repository or many code repositories.

- Information moves between parts of the system over a network, often via HTTP, RPC (Remote Procedure Call), or queuing systems.

- Data contracts must be intentionally designed and well thought out, as contracts are implemented as APIs and communicated over a network.

## CHOOSING BETWEEN A SERVICE-ORIENTED ARCHITECTURE AND A MONOLITH

In general, a monolith is easier to set up than an SOA and requires considerably fewer technical logistics to manage. For this reason, a monolith is the right answer on day one for the vast majority of problems. If the team is very disciplined and thoughtful about designing a monolith, it can scale with the team forever. This won't be the case for everyone, however. For many teams/projects, a monolith's lack of enforced contracts, inability to scale as separate components, and lack of enforced separation of concerns will become a barrier to productivity.

If you do find yourself contending with an unruly monolith, this doesn't mean your engineers are bad at their jobs. The nature of software engineering is that requirements change and systems evolve. Maintaining a monolith may mean, at times, investing considerable resources into updating the system design to evolve as well, and it is when a team fails to make this investment that monolith complexity becomes a barrier to productivity.

There are some circumstances where moving to a service-oriented architecture is clearly the right choice:

- Your service has elements that need to be scaled independently. For example, one feature consumes lots of CPU resources and you don't want that to interfere with other features, or you prefer not to pay to scale up all features when it's more cost-effective to scale that one piece independently.

- You're working on functionality that needs to expose its own independent API and has its own exclusive data domain apart from the main system. Especially if this API is meant to serve external customers, then having this functionality live as its own service is an obvious good choice.

- For some reason, you need to use another programming language as part of your application. A good example might be because there is a robust and high-quality framework for solving a certain kind of problem in Python, but the rest of your application is in Java. Bridging these two languages in memory is possible, but clunky. The easier option is to bridge them via an API, leaving them naturally hosted as separate services.

- Deploying your monolith is overly expensive, slow, or risky. In this case, you can enable additional productivity and reduce time to deploy by deploying new code as an independent service. Just ensure that the new service operates independent of the monolith and you're not creating new deployment dependencies.

## Source Control for Service-Oriented Architectures: monorepo and manyrepo

Managing source code for a monolith is fairly straightforward because it lives in a single repository with a single-build system. Once you start to break out your code into different packages, projects, and services, you're faced with a decision: do you manage multiple services in a single code repository, or do you make multiple repositories? This tradeoff is referred to as monorepo vs. manyrepo.

If you choose to manage multiple services as a monorepo you'll likely want to look for a workspace management solution (e.g., yarn workspaces for JavaScript ecosystem) to manage building the projects separately. Here are some basic differences between the monorepo and manyrepo approaches:

**Pros and cons of monorepo**

- It's easy to ensure every service or package dependency is up to date with the latest version.
- Many CI systems do not support multiple packages in a single repo natively, so you have to build a harness manually to support this.
- Having all the code in a single repository improves discoverability, making it easier for developers to find the module or reference they're looking for. IDEs have robust support for this kind of search.

**Manyrepo, by contrast**

- Requires using a central package manager with version control. This isn't necessarily a bad thing, but it can lead to significant overhead when working on a project and its dependencies simultaneously.
- Integrates cleanly with CI/CD pipeline systems (Bitbucket pipelines, GitHub actions, etc.).

My general advice is to keep things simple. For small-to-medium-sized projects, a monorepo will be simpler to set up and maintain. Transitioning to manyrepo means being willing to make an investment in tooling to ensure manyrepo works smoothly for your developers; it's a significant cost. For a small startup, that cost is likely not worth it. On the flip side, if you're growing rapidly or are passing fifty-plus developers, and monorepo is becoming unwieldy, and you've got a dedicated internal platform or DevOps team that can do the heavy lifting of making manyrepo easy to use, then transitioning to a manyrepo pattern may be the right choice.

## THE DISTRIBUTED MONOLITH

A distributed monolith is a system deployed as multiple services that are not designed with sufficient independence or isolation and thus are not independently deployable. To be clear, this is the worst of both worlds. Rather than enabling a developer to go to any service and to work on it in isolation, not thinking about any other service, this setup requires that developer to reason about how that service affects other services. Not only that, but they have to then make changes potentially in multiple services and coordinate deployments in a particular order between services to ensure compatibility during releases. This development and deployment complexity negates the key benefits of a microservice system.

If you notice your team falling into these patterns or complaining about coordinating releases between services, this should be a red flag for you to look closer and consider paying down some tech debt to get back to independently deployable services. That tech debt is usually located in your contracts, the design of your APIs, and how data is handled in your system.

## WRITING READABLE, "GOOD" CODE

In a professional environment, the principal audience for any given line of code is not the computer but the developer who has to read that code at some point in the future for further development. This is the golden rule of programming: engineers should be writing code with the same level of readability that they expect of anyone else's code.

## CHOICE OF LANGUAGE AND ECOSYSTEM

Per the golden rule of programming, your choice of language should enable your team to write code that is highly readable and maintainable. In general, a good engineer can do that in any language; however, some languages make it easier than others to do so consistently. Some other considerations for what language or ecosystem to choose:

- How large is the talent pool that is familiar with that language, and—more specifically—is familiar with that environment and also interested in startups like yours?

- Are there existing implementations that you can use as a starting point?

- Do you have particular performance or scaling requirements? Some languages are much faster than others for specific types of tasks. Haskell is famously inefficient at string manipulation, and C is famously fast at most things, though there are other languages that, for certain problems, approach or exceed the speed of C while providing an easier and more friendly coding environment.

- Is there a particular framework that might be a good starting point in a particular language? React Native, for example, is a powerful cross-platform mobile language that requires JavaScript or TypeScript.

In the enterprise setting, I recommend languages with static type systems, such as Golang, TypeScript, Rust, etc., so that the compiler can do more heavy lifting for ensuring code correctness, so that those constraints are visible to other developers, and so you don't run into that category of issue at runtime. You should strive for a local development environment where the tools are finding errors before your code is executed, called compile time checks. Fixing a compile time check is in general much faster and cheaper than fixing a runtime issue, and also—by virtue of the fact that it's automated—is better equipped than a runtime check to reliably find problems.

## CODE STYLE AND FORMATTING

In any widely used language, there will be either a published standard for how code should be formatted (e.g., PEP8 in Python) or a configurable tool that can enforce a particular code style and formatting (e.g., ESLint or Prettier in JavaScript, or ReSharper in C#). Most of these tools are very good at ensuring that code, regardless of who wrote it, is stylistically identical. In the spirit of ensuring your codebase is readable, there is no excuse for not using one of these tools and ensuring 100 percent of your codebase is formatted according to the same rules. Which rules you use is entirely you and your team's preference, but just make sure it's consistent and produces a readable result.

I recommend you have a set of configuration options or instructions for the integrated development environments (IDEs) your developers use on how to auto format code when a file is saved. You should then, in your continuous integration system, ensure that all new code is formatted correctly. Be careful: enforcing style in your continuous integration system without automatic formatting is very frustrating for engineers, so make sure to train everyone in setting up their IDE correctly on day one to avoid consistent surprises and wasted cycle time from lint failures in CI.

## STATIC CODE ANALYSIS

Modern static code analysis is capable of identifying and alerting on a wide range of common code issues, ranging from security gaps to outright bugs to stylistic inconsistencies. These tools are fairly inexpensive and integrate neatly with a wide range of commonly used continuous integration systems and developer IDEs. From experience using these tools on a range of projects and programming languages, the signal-to-noise ratio is very good, and the output is a net gain in productivity and software quality. Relatively early on in your software project's life, you should integrate static code analysis. I encourage you to look at tools that are specific both to your programming language of choice—e.g., ESLint for JavaScript—as well as generic analysis platforms such as SonarCloud, Codebeat, Scrutinizer-CI, Code Climate, or Cloudacity.

## Greenfield vs. Brownfield

Greenfield software development refers to development work in a new environment with minimal pre-existing legacy code and free choice on tools, patterns, and architecture. This has the obvious advantage of allowing the thoughtful choice of the right architecture and tooling for the job, and no distraction from existing tech debt. The subtle downside is that, with so much choice and so few constraints, the risks of making poor decisions are higher. There is also usually a considerable bootstrap cost for new projects that is underestimated— things like setting up testing, build systems, static code analysis, etc.

Brownfield software development refers to the opposite of greenfield, working with existing legacy systems. The tradeoffs are essentially inverted: for better or worse, you're stuck with the high-level decisions that have been made by those before you.

The largest risk in brownfield development is "not invented here" syndrome. "Not invented here" is the tendency for individuals to avoid taking responsibility for or paying sufficient attention to things they did not create themselves. In brownfield software development, this can lead to systematic underinvestment in understanding existing work, causing frustration and inefficiency in augmenting or modifying existing systems. I strongly encourage managers to make explicit space for a team to read and understand an existing system before asking them to modify it in any way. The time spent in comprehension upfront will be paid back by fewer surprises and faster velocity down the road.

### 3.1 ARCHITECTURE

## CODING PATTERNS

The subject of what style of code to write is a religious discussion for many coders. My intention in this chapter is to provide a brief description of what the most common phrases in coding patterns mean, and refer you to more extensive resources on each practice.

If you're faced with what feels like an emotional conversation on this topic, keep in mind that many successful companies exist that use each of these patterns. Everything is a tradeoff. A bad programmer can make a mess with any tool, and conversely a great programmer will find a way to make a readable solution even with suboptimal tools.

## OBJECT-ORIENTED PROGRAMMING (OOP)

Object-oriented programming (OOP) is a methodology of designing code to mirror real-world nouns and verbs. A typical example would be to model an interaction between two people as two Person objects, and any actions for people, such as talking, would be functions on those objects. Many languages are inherently object-oriented, such as Python, Ruby, and C#. Some, like JavaScript or C++, are "Object-Optional" (supporting to an extent both object-oriented and functional styles) and others are something else entirely.

## PURITY

Code that is "pure" has no external dependencies or side effects. Said another way, given the same inputs, a pure piece of code will always produce the same outputs. The advantage of pure code is that it is easily testable and requires no external setup or mocking. Pure code is also easier to read and understand, as it does not require reading any additional code to understand what it does. A simple example of pure code would be a function that sums together two numbers; given any two input numbers, the sum function always produces the same output.

Some code is inherently impure—for example, code that interacts with the outside world, such as a filesystem, network, or database. For most other scenarios it's possible to model business logic in a pure way. Where possible, I encourage you and your team to write pure code.

## FUNCTIONAL PROGRAMMING

To stick with the parts-of-speech model for describing coding patterns, functional programming treats verbs (functions) as a first-class part of the system. Most functional programming starts with very tiny pieces of functionality and composes it together to create more sophisticated and complex systems. When it's done well, the benefit of functional code is that it tends to be more pure, and thus easier to read, reason about, and test in isolation. Academic examples of functional code even exist that can be formally reasoned about, meaning one can produce a mathematical proof that code runs correctly.

Functional programming, done poorly, can create very verbose and hard-to-read code. For example, when composing together multiple functions, it's important to consider how many functions are being composed, and how obvious the behavior of each function is in the composition chain. A worst-case scenario: Imagine a function chain of ten functions in a row, each with names that have no meaning to you (e.g., "a(b(c(d(e(f(g(h(i(j(input)))))))))))"). The only thing worse would be if the definitions of these alphabet functions were in ten different files in different places of the codebase, or worse, came from different imported libraries.

## EXTREME PROGRAMMING AND TEST-DRIVEN DEVELOPMENT (TDD)

Extreme programming is a development methodology, akin to Agile or SCRUM. It may be used to reference the formal methodology described in the book *Extreme Programming Explained* by Kent Beck, or more informally to address some of the coding practices espoused by the methodology. The informal usage of the phrase describes the testing practices in the methodology, specifically the idea of test-driven development.

Test-driven development (TDD) is a process where tests are written before functional software, as opposed to writing functional code first and tests after. Behavior-driven development (BDD) and acceptance-test driven development (ATDD) are similar practices.

## DEPENDENCY INJECTION

Dependency injection is a pattern where the service dependencies of a particular object, module, or block of code are passed in, rather than instantiated. For example, a data object can instantiate its own connection to a database by looking up a connection string in a configuration file and creating the database client. Alternatively, a parent-calling block of code can create the database service, then pass the single database service into each instance of the data object.

The main advantage of dependency injection is that it decreases the coupling between a service and its dependencies, effectively adding a documented interface between them. This interface allows, for example, other implementations of the interface to be used, such as a mock service in a testing context.

There are subtleties inherent to doing dependency injection cleanly. I encourage you to adopt frameworks or patterns that are commonly used and well thought out for your programming language.

## DOMAIN-DRIVEN DESIGN

The term "Domain-Driven Design" comes from a book by Eric Evans, *Domain-Driven Design*, published in 2003. The core idea is to create a model—be it for objects in object-oriented design or for a schema for your database—that models the nouns in your business domain. This may seem simple and intuitive; however, with complex business domains, it's easy for code either to inconsistently model the domain, or to model it in a way that hinders comprehension by the team. Especially with larger and more complex problems, I always insist that the team sit down and agree on a consistent way to model the problem, using consistent terminology to refer to the same concepts across the entire system.

## API CONTRACTS

An application programming interface (API) is not unlike a legal contract. It is designed, tweaked, and agreed upon in advance of implementation, and both parties expect the other to conform to the contract to achieve a desired outcome. When you design and implement an API, you're making a commitment to the consumers of your API that it will work in a certain way. Like a legal contract, you may have a specific idea of how your API will function, but if the nuances are interpreted differently by the other party, you may be unable to achieve your purpose. API details truly do matter, and as a technical leader it's your role to ensure that your team is designing and building APIs in a consistent, efficient manner.

All that said, building a high-quality API is a surprisingly complex task. It requires taking into account many things: designing the interface, implementing the code that handles the logic/data, testing the functionality, building the documentation, addressing versioning/change management, keeping the documentation up to date as the API changes, and making it easy for developers to interact with the API. Doing these things well can mean the difference between building an API that developers love and an API that stymies implementation and slows down time to launch important projects. There are two main levers at your disposal as a leader to ensure you're handling these things well: governance and architecture.

## API DESIGN GOVERNANCE

Countless decisions go into every element of building an API. What separates "good" APIs from "bad" APIs is the consistency, predictability, and correctness of those decisions. As a technical leader the job falls on you to make sure that, across your organization, you have a structure in place to help developers build APIs that are consistent with one another, predictable in that they use common patterns that are appropriate for the problem at hand, and correct.

Achieving these goals requires some form of governance system. This can range from a set of clearly documented guidelines and standards to a group of people who are responsible for reviewing and approving all APIs on a regular basis. The larger your team, the more time and effort you'll need to invest in process and governance to maintain a high standard.

## API ARCHITECTURE

Out in the wild you're likely to encounter two main types of APIs: HTTP-based and non-HTTP based. As with any tool, HTTP has its tradeoffs and isn't ideal for every job, so if your business requirements dictate ultra-low latency, or ultra-high throughput/low overhead, or real-time streaming applications, you'll likely be looking for something beyond HTTP. Below I discuss a handful of HTTP API types and then briefly cover some non-HTTP APIs you're likely to run into.

### HTTP-Based APIs

If you're building a web or mobile application, or even most system back-ends, chances are very high you'll primarily be dealing with HTTP APIs.

#### XML and SOAP APIs

In the early 2000s, the most common API pattern was the XML-based Simple Object Access Protocol (SOAP). SOAP and other XML-based API styles are well and truly out of fashion with startups in the 2020s, but they are still prevalent in legacy systems, especially from larger companies in technologically slow-moving industries. You should not be building new SOAP or XML-based APIs.

#### REST

REST (Representational State Transfer) is a generic phrase that describes using JSON over HTTP as an API. REST is sometimes augmented with a pattern called HATEOAS, which provides a more formal set of standards to the content/payloads of a REST API. Absent HATEOAS (which isn't all that common), REST does not include formal or branded guidance for how JSON data is modeled. REST APIs commonly model a single noun as an endpoint and use HTTP verbs (GET, PUT, POST, DELETE, etc.) to determine actions on nouns. For example, GET/users would list users, POST/users would create a new user, and DELETE/users/123 would delete the user with ID 123.

REST is likely the most common form of API you'll encounter. REST has a broad and robust tool ecosystem and nearly every engineer is familiar with it.

## GraphQL

GraphQL is similar to REST in that it's JSON over HTTP; however, it does not rely on HTTP verbs. Nearly everything on GraphQL is a POST, and it uses a structured schema of queries and mutations.

I like to think of GraphQL as REST with types and a self-documenting schema. As a result, GraphQL APIs tend to come with automatically generated documentation and schema explorers. GraphQL also, by virtue of its schema system, allows for the composition of multiple schemas from multiple services to form a larger, more powerful, and more complex data graph, sometimes called a federated schema. The company Apollo provides sophisticated solutions for managing and scaling a graph.

There's a lot to be said for the benefits of building a graph to model your company's data, and the good habits that being forced to design a schema bring about. That said, no system comes without tradeoffs. Because GraphQL forgoes standard HTTP verbs, it does not play nicely with some elements of the web stack. GET request caching and developer tooling are still catching up to deal nicely with GraphQL requests. If those drawbacks are not a significant concern for your business, I strongly encourage you to check out apollographql.com and consider using GraphQL—especially for internal use cases—for your APIs.

## Non-HTTP APIs

In general, for traditional synchronous request/response- (aka remote procedure call or RPC-) style APIs, you'll want to use an HTTP API due to its ubiquitous nature. However, there are several API patterns—especially for asynchronous operations—that don't map neatly to HTTP and have commonly used alternative implementations.

### Queueing systems

A queueing system maintains an inbox (or set of inboxes) to receive messages and an interface for a consumer to read messages with certain guarantees. A typical queueing system can guarantee message order (either first in first out, FIFO; or last in first out, LIFO) as well as "at least once" or "at most once" delivery. Most cloud platforms have hosted implementations of queues, such as AWS Simple Queue Service (SQS) or Google Cloud Task queues.

Queueing systems often have a notion of *explicit* invocation, which is to say that when a publisher creates a message, it explicitly specifies how the request should be handled or executed. By contrast, most publisher–subscriber systems support *implicit* execution. This means publishers do not necessarily know beforehand what system will handle the message, only that the pub/sub system will deliver it.

### Publisher-Subscriber ("pub/sub") Pattern

The publisher-subscriber pattern, abbreviated as pub/sub, allows for designing a system where messages are created by potentially multiple sources and delivered via various patterns to potentially multiple subscribers. Publisher-subscriber relationships are modeled as one-to-one (direct), one-to-many (fan-out), many-to-one (fan-in), and many-to-many. Various pub/sub implementations can provide guarantees that messages are delivered to all subscribers, at least one subscriber, at least one time, etc. Similar to queues, there are off-the-shelf solutions, such as RabbitMQ, as well as easily scaled cloud-hosted options like Amazon Simple Notification Service (SNS) or Google Cloud Pub/Sub.

The pub/sub pattern and the guarantees it provides are extremely powerful. However, the tradeoff is that implementations require some care and attention to detail to realize the advertised guarantees. Implementing a subscriber, for example, requires paying close attention to message acknowledgement semantics and carefully managing topic subscriptions to ensure the right messages go to the right place.

If you're torn between implementing a solution with queues, pub/sub, or an HTTP API, my general recommendation is to keep it simple and go with the synchronous HTTP API. The fact that you are torn between implementations indicates that the guarantees offered by the asynchronous systems are not critical to your implementation, and therefore the added complexity is likely not worth it for your startup project.

## Job Systems

Jobs, or cron jobs, are a type of backend API that are rarely triggered by a publisher or client, but instead by some form of timer. Common examples include nightly data cleanup tasks, or sending weekly email summaries/notifications. Some best practices for jobs:

- Use a job system maintained by somebody else, don't build one yourself.

- When choosing a job system (or building one yourself, if you must), ensure that it

    o has logging for every job execution;

    o allows for configuring the retrying of jobs that fail;

    o provides notification when jobs fail. It's very common for engineers to set up a scheduled job, watch it work on day one, and then on day fifteen it fails and nobody notices until day thirty;

    o provides an interface to view jobs and job status;

    o allows for job configuration to be stored as code or configuration in source control;

    o allows for jobs to be run inside your environment/private networks/security groups as necessary to access other internal system APIs/resources;

    o integrates with your secret management system.

    o allows for easily setting up jobs locally in development and production environments, and easy testing in each of those environments.

## DOCUMENTATION

Having thorough, clear, and current documentation for your API is just as critical as how you build and maintain it. Some key characteristics of great API documentation:

- Always up to date with the implementation

- Documents all possible inputs and their types

- Documents all possible errors

- Easily read and navigated by other engineers

It's always a good idea to build your API using a system that includes API documentation generation. Doing otherwise means it'll be practically impossible to meet all of these goals on a consistent basis. If you're building a REST API, I strongly encourage you to design your API using OpenAPI (a YAML or JSON document that describes your API). In most languages there are SDKs to consume an OpenAPI spec and automatically generate controllers/routes to match the spec and/or generate a test harness to ensure the implemented API matches the spec. In addition, there are online tools, such as stoplight.io and readme.com, that can consume OpenAPI documents and generate aesthetically pleasing and easy-to-navigate documentation.

If you're using GraphQL, the GraphQL Playground or Apollo Studio explorer can provide a reasonable stand-in for extensive type documentation. I do recommend you still build a separate API documentation page, either using a tool like readme.com or creating something by hand, to act as a primer or getting started guide. The built-in GraphQL documentation lacks a description of how authentication works, and it also does a poor job of providing space to explain the relationships between data in your API. These are gaps you need to fill elsewhere.

Another benefit of using either OpenAPI or GraphQL is that the resulting API specification is portable not only to documentation generators and test frameworks but also to developer IDEs such as Insomnia or Postman. These IDEs enable developers to quickly interact with an API to validate functionality without writing code. Formal specifications can also be used with code generation tools to ensure typing consistency in code.

## IDEMPOTENCY

An API request is said to be idempotent when making the same request multiple times has the same effect as making it a single time. Idempotency is an important concept in building robust systems and avoiding data corruption. As with all things, idempotency gives you useful guarantees about a system but it comes with a cost: implementing idempotency adds complexity to backend systems.

In REST APIs, it is widely assumed that every HTTP verb except POST should be idempotent. GET requests, for example, by definition should always return the same result for the same input (unless the underlying data changes, of course). In general, PUT requests are modifying existing objects and should naturally be idempotent. Multiple calls to a POST request, however, in most systems signal the intention to create multiple objects.

### Idempotency Keys

For HTTP POST requests in REST and for GraphQL mutation APIs, idempotency is not provided by the standard/specification. If you want a client to be able to retry these kinds of requests and have idempotent behavior, you should implement the idempotency key pattern. An idempotency key is an arbitrary string, provided by the client (either as an HTTP header or perhaps in GraphQL as an input variable), that backends use to de-duplicate incoming requests. This requires the backend to store the idempotency key, and also store the response to a request with that key, to be provided to clients later on.

Note that implementing an idempotency key is non-trivial, as it will require additional database writes, logic around capturing request responses, and dealing with concurrency/locking issues for duplicate requests that arrive at the same time. If idempotency is important in your application—say, if you're dealing with financial transactions—I encourage you to adopt a backend API implementation that provides a robust idempotency system out of the box rather than building it yourself from scratch.

## DATA AND ANALYTICS

Most startups have at least three different kinds of data they use as part of their business:

- Transactional data

- Analytical business intelligence data

- Behavioral data

Each of these types of data will come in different volumes, have different read/write patterns, and require different tools to visualize and glean insights.

A quick note on the phrase "big data." As a startup, the chances are very good that you do *not* have big data in the sense that it needs to be architected with infinity-scale (or "web scale") in mind. Typical off-the-shelf databases with reasonable quantities of hardware and half-decent data model design are more than capable of handling tens of millions of rows and hundreds of gigabytes of data with acceptable performance. Most big data solutions, such as data pipelines or data warehouse appliances, involve significant added setup complexity, latency, and cost, and they're likely overkill for your startup. For the sake of simplicity, big data solutions should only be considered if you can make a compelling argument that a regular (e.g., PostgreSQL) database cannot do the job. Said another way, don't prematurely optimize your database architecture.

## TRANSACTIONAL DATA

Transactional data is the data that powers your application itself, typically your primary NoSQL or SQL database. Transactional data requires very low latency and high availability, and is modest in total size compared to the other forms of data. My recommendation is to choose an off-the-shelf SQL or NoSQL solution, preferably something hosted for you such as MongoDB Atlas or Google Cloud SQL. Some nice-to-haves in your production database:

- One-click point-in-time restore

- Regular backups with one-click restore

- Read-only replicas for load shedding

- Multi-zone replication and hosting for availability

- Event-based audit logging

- Automated disk expansion/contraction

- Connection/IP-level security

- Resource (CPU, RAM, Disk, Network) monitoring and alerting

- One-click scaling up/down for CPU/RAM

- Slow query monitoring

## ANALYTICAL BUSINESS INTELLIGENCE DATA

Business intelligence (BI) is data that is used to gain insight into behaviors of your users, usually sourced from your transactional data. Early on, you can often get away with running business intelligence queries directly on your transactional database. As the size of data and query complexity increase, this becomes more problematic as it adds additional load to a system that requires high availability and low latency. The natural solution then is either to query a read-only replica of your transactional database, or copy/transform the data to another data storage system via a data pipeline.

Building data pipelines and data warehousing is an entire book unto itself, and the state of the art is always evolving. I have just a few high-level bits of advice:

- Consider looking at enterprise data solutions like Snowflake, Databricks, or Google BigQuery for your primary business intelligence data warehouse. These tools are game changers. The serverless warehouses in particular (BigQuery, Aurora) are trivial to set up, have fairly consistent latency regardless of data size, and are highly cost-effective for early/mid-stage startups.

- In modern times, a startup doesn't need to build and host sophisticated data pipeline architectures. ELT (Extract, Load, Transform) and ETL (Extract, Transform, Load) tools can now run entirely inside an enterprise database data lake/warehouse, and tools such as dbt provide reproducibility, testability, and pipeline-as-code capabilities, making running data pipelines much more manageable.

- Consider using hosted or cloud-native solutions for visualizing data such as Looker, Domo, or Preset.

- Make sure your engineering and product teams are collaborating closely with whichever member of your team owns data and business intelligence. Bringing in data's perspective early in the product process will save a lot of headache down the road with a "measure twice, create-data-schema once" mindset.

## BEHAVIORAL DATA

Behavioral data—also called behavioral analytics events—describes how users have used your application. Behavioral data is often fairly high volume, with a somewhat limited schema, and is best used in combination with powerful visualization software.

Overall, you'll want behavioral data from your application to go to multiple sources. This presents a bit of a routing problem: you have a single data source (your application), but you want events to go to many places. The nearly universally adopted solution to this problem is Twilio's Segment platform, though there are some up-and-coming alternatives called Customer Data Platforms (CDP) such as RudderStack. A CDP can ingest data from your application, then send it to your data warehouse and to as many other SaaS platforms as you like.

One important distinction between behavioral data generated by your application and transactional data is its precision. Most behavioral data is lossy—users have ad blockers, requests get dropped, or firewalls get in the way. There are many reasons why events might not make it from a client device to your CDP. That doesn't mean behavioral data is not useful, but being aware of its lossiness should inform your expectations for the data and limit the use cases when querying it. If you need exact numbers, expect to derive those from your BI platform and your transactional data.

## GENERAL TIPS AND BEST PRACTICES FOR ARCHITECTURE DESIGN

Let's close out this section with a few overall recommendations for designing your architecture.

## PUT BUSINESS LOGIC IN THE BACKEND

As you build out your application you're often confronted with the choice of where logic should live: on the client (e.g., web browser, mobile device, physical hardware) or some form of backend server. For certain types of logic, such as anything related to authentication, value calculations, anti-cheating/tampering mechanisms, this is a firm requirement. For most other logic it's still a good idea for the following reasons:

- Backends are often easier to test than clients, so you can more confidently confirm the correctness of business logic on the backend.

- More logic on the backend means thinner clients, and also means you can produce clients for multiple platforms that can leverage a single source for logic, reducing code duplication.

- Logic on the backend can't be tampered with or modified by the client.

## MAKE SERVICES EXTERNALIZABLE

The APIs from your backend to other backends, or your backend to frontends, should be thought of as generic-purpose APIs that could be consumed by third parties. This forces you to maintain several good design habits, including ensuring that interfaces are comprehensible on their own (domain-driven design), and using sensible authentication mechanisms and appropriate high-level ownership abstractions in data design. And, on the off chance you do one day wish to externalize a service, the road to doing so will be much shorter.

## USE AS FEW LANGUAGES AS POSSIBLE

With every programming language comes an associated build system, dependency management system, programming best practices, and interfaces. Your team should be putting in considerable effort to ensure your primary language and ecosystem are well integrated and working well for local developers, test environments, and production environments.

For every additional language you add to your stack, you'll need to replicate all of that effort, and you'll suffer from an inability to share code between the runtimes. Before allowing an additional language in your stack you should be able to build a robust and bulletproof argument that the benefits of the new language dwarf the operational and maintenance burdens that the new language adds. Otherwise you're better off without it.

# 3.2 Tools

The tooling ecosystem and patterns for software engineering are constantly evolving and changing. You will inevitably be tempted either on your own or by members of your team to change something about how you're doing engineering, such as adopting a new library, framework, language, or pattern. Adopting each of these changes quickly leads to a patchwork quilt of poorly thought-out architecture. Conversely, ignoring all change leaves you with a stale codebase that, over time, will be less efficient and harder for newly hired talent to work on. The right approach is to formalize the process of changing your tech stack and provide some guardrails to motivate your team to be curious and thoughtful about tooling changes.

## IMPLEMENTING INTERNAL TECHNOLOGY RADAR

Thoughtworks, a leading software consultancy based out of San Francisco, publishes a tool called the Technology Radar (ctohb.com/radar) that evaluates the hundreds of projects Thoughtworks sees every year. They put new tools, techniques, patterns, and languages (which they call blips) in one of four categories based on how effective they are in the real world. The categories are hold, assess, trial, and adopt.

If you've never read through a Thoughtworks Radar, I highly recommend it as a general primer on what's going on, and also as inspiration for your own team's process.

My preferred way to balance the challenge of keeping engineers motivated and a codebase relevant with tool churn is to follow Thoughtworks' lead and implement an internal technology radar. Rather than weigh something new for its universal appeal as Thoughtworks does, my approach evaluates blips for their fit and effectiveness for our organization using the same four levels. To be concrete:

1. Somebody proposes using a new tool, technique, platform, or language (blip). That proposal at first is categorized as "assess." The proposer has to make the case in a technical document that the new blip would provide a material benefit to the project that was already selected by the business (or as an experiment in an innovation sprint—see Cooldown/ Innovation Sprints, page 163). Then, if approved, it moves to a trial.

2. The new blip is used by the developer in a project, either selected by the business or in their innovation sprint window. At the end of the project, the author produces a follow-up written document describing their experience with the blip, including pros and cons and how well the blip plays with the rest of the tooling ecosystem at the company.

3. Based on the results of the trial, the team as a whole will move to either adopt the blip, unlocking that blip to be used by the rest of the team

without further ceremony, or move it to "hold," which would require a new trial and a new evaluation for it to be used again. If a trial fails in a business project, the team is advised to think carefully about whether to remove the blip from that implementation to avoid future maintenance concerns.

In most cases, I find that when a blip trial fails, it fails relatively early on and the engineer leading the project doesn't include the blip in the final delivered implementation.

## Boring Technology

"Boring Technology" is a phrase coined by Dan McKinley and outlined at ctohb.com/boring. The key idea is that your team's job is to deliver functionality to support the business, and most of the time that doesn't depend on using fancy new tools. In fact, using something that's "not boring" often has many hidden costs, and only if your team is fully cognizant of those costs and believes the benefits are larger, should the new tool be adopted. As Boring Technology describes it, "total cost = maintenance cost - velocity benefit." Some hidden costs to consider:

- Incomplete, inaccurate, or immature documentation
- Not fully developed ecosystems around the tool/technology, including SDKs and integrations with other tools
- A higher likelihood of encountering defects or missing functionality/features
- Additional training cost for members of your team to adopt the new tool
- Burden in keeping that tool or package up to date, patching security holes, etc.

## TOOL COST

It's a fact of life that modern startups will spend a lot on SaaS. Your company is likely no exception, so don't be surprised when you find you are spending an entire headcount or more on infrastructure and tools before your Series B fundraise.

### BUDGET

There are a handful of published benchmarks for SaaS and tool spend at various company stages as a percentage of either company revenue or total spend. There's not a single precise benchmark, but it seems that typical SaaS Costs of Goods Sold (COGS) fall somewhere between 10 and 30 percent of revenue.

Know your spend and keep an eye on cost growth. It's very easy to accidentally leave a couple of machines running in AWS and add $10,000 to your annual cloud hosting bills. Most cloud platforms have built-in budgeting features, so there's no excuse to not use them. If you're using infrastructure as code, it's easy to set up a module that, for every new cloud system deployed, will automatically apply a cloud budget at the same time that will monitor and alert on cost for that particular system.

It's typical for SaaS costs to grow over time, be it because your infrastructure is growing, or because you discover a new SaaS vendor that can save your team time. I recommend not using cost as a reason to avoid adopting a typical SaaS tool (with a cost range in the hundreds per month). Instead, I'd advise factoring regular growth into your SaaS cost forecasts.

### TRACKING

You should be tracking how much your organization spends on engineering tools, including IDEs, SaaS, and infrastructure (cloud platforms). You can do this manually in a spreadsheet or using a SaaS Management Platform (SMP). Available from various vendors such as BetterCloud, Zluri, and Vendr, these solutions link with your credit card or bank and automatically categorize cash spend.

# 3.3 DevOps

Wikipedia describes DevOps as "a set of practices that combines software development and IT operations. It aims to shorten the systems development lifecycle and provide continuous delivery with high software quality."

I translate that as follows: DevOps is all the work that goes into making sure the business software runs in places other than your developers' machines. Unless you've got a DevOps specialist on your team, you're probably deprioritizing DevOps to some degree, and have underinvested in it as well. It's not just my opinion; it's becoming widely accepted throughout tech industries that high-quality DevOps is a key driver of overall engineering velocity.

## FOUR KEY METRICS (DORA)

The highest-rated blip in 2022 of the Thoughtworks Technology Radar (ctohb.com/techradar) is the Four Key Metrics. These metrics are described by a team within Google Cloud called DORA (DevOps Research and Assessment), and the system of metrics comes from a seven-plus-year research program validating the results and their impact on technology, process, culture, and quantitative results. The four metrics are as follows:

- **Lead Time:** How long it takes for code to go from commit to running in production

- **Deployment Frequency:** How often code is released to production/end users

- **Mean Time to Recovery (MTTR):** How long it takes to restore service after an incident/defect occurs

- **Change Fail Percentage:** What percentage of production releases need a hotfix, rollback, patch, etc

Together these metrics quantify the idea of how confidently your team can deploy software. Scoring high on all four metrics requires an investment in automation, DevOps, testing, and culture. As Thoughtworks is quick to point out, drawing value from these metrics doesn't necessarily require highly detailed instrumentation, metrics, or dashboards. DORA publishes a quick check survey (ctohb.com/dora) that your team can take to track its progress at a coarse-grained level. There are also plenty of tools that have fairly low barriers to entry that will yield data quality that's more than sufficient to inform your progress, such as LinearB or Code Climate.

The following subsections on DevOps present concepts, disciplines, and focus areas that contribute in some way to improving these metrics.

## REPRODUCIBILITY

Deploying code is a highly nuanced activity that requires extreme precision. A single misplaced character in a configuration file can lead to a service failing to start. Worse still, debugging DevOps problems for most engineers is slow and painful, and identifying and fixing that single character error can mean potentially hours of time lost in debugging and fixing. We're all human; these kinds of errors are inevitable. Since they're so expensive in DevOps, it is imperative that we put systems in place to minimize the opportunity for human error. A key component of minimizing the frequency and impact of human error in DevOps is the concept of reproducibility.

Reproducibility implies that we have the capability of doing something a second time that is both inexpensive and guaranteed to be identical to how it was done the first time. Reproducibility in DevOps requires automation and tooling. Arguably, the most important tool in the DevOps tool belt for improving reproducibility and accelerating development time is containerization. A close second is the idea of Infrastructure as Code (IaC). Since these techniques are so fundamental, I'll spend a bit of time introducing each of them here.

## CONTAINERIZATION

The most common way of explaining the role of containers in the DevOps context is to consider where the name originated: from shipping containers. Prior to the standardization of shipping containers, if you wanted to transport goods across the ocean, you would package your cargo in a variety of forms ranging from placing it on pallets, storing it in boxes or barrels, or simply wrapping it in cloth. Loading and unloading goods that arrived packaged in all these different ways was inefficient and error-prone, mainly because there's no single kind of crane or wheelbarrow that could effectively move all of the cargo.

Compare that haphazard approach to deploying a standardized shipping container where the boat and port operator can work with a single form factor, using standardized equipment and shippers and a single, flexible form of packaging for all of their goods. Historically, the usage of standardized shipping containers unlocked a paradigm shift that reduced costs of global shipping by orders of magnitude. Packaging software in a standardized container that can be run on any system in the same way provides an analogous advancement in capability and efficiency.

The most common way you'll interact with containers is through a software system called Docker. Docker provides a declarative programming language that lets you describe, in a file called Dockerfile, how you want the system set up—i.e., what programs need to be installed, what files go where, what dependencies need to exist. Then you build that file into a container image which provides a representation of the entire file system specified by your Dockerfile. That image can then be moved to and run on any other machine with a Docker-compatible container runtime, with the guarantee that it will start in an isolated environment with the exact same files and data, every time.

## CONTAINER MANAGEMENT BEST PRACTICES

### Design Containers to Build Once/Run Anywhere

Build the container once (say, in CI) so that it can run in your various environments—production, development, etc. By using a single image, you guarantee that exactly the same code with exactly the same setup will transition intact from development to production.

To achieve run-anywhere with your containers, extract any differences between environments to runtime container environmental variables. These are secrets and configurations like connection strings or hostnames. Alternatively, you can implement an entrypoint script in your image that downloads the necessary configuration and secrets from a central secret store (e.g., Amazon or Google Secret Manager, HashiCorp Vault, etc.) before invoking your application.

An additional benefit to the runtime secret/configuration download strategy is that it's reusable for local development, avoiding the need for developers to ever manually fetch secrets or ask another developer to send them the secret file.

## Build Images in CI

In the spirit of reproducibility, I encourage you to build your images using automation, preferably part of continuous integration. This ensures the images are themselves built in a repeatable way.

## Use a Hosted Registry

Once you're building container images and moving them around, you'll immediately want to be organized about managing the built images themselves. I recommend tagging each image with a unique value derived from source control, perhaps also with a timestamp (e.g., the git hash of the commit where the image was built), and hosting the image in an image registry. Dockerhub has a private registry product, and all the major cloud platforms also offer hosted image registries.

Many hosted registries will also provide vulnerability scanning and other security features attached to their image registry.

## Keep Image Sizes as Small as Possible

Smaller Docker images upload faster from CI, download faster to application servers, and start up faster. The difference between uploading a 50MB image and a 5GB image, from an operational perspective, can be the difference between five seconds to start up a new application server and five minutes. That's five more minutes added to your time to deploy, Mean Time to Recovery/rollback, etc. It may not seem like much, but— especially in a hotfix scenario, or when you're managing hundreds of application servers—these delays add up and have real business impact.

## Dockerfile Best Practices

Every "line" or "command" in a Dockerfile generates what is called a layer—effectively, a snapshot of the entire image's hard disk. Subsequent layers store deltas between layers. A container image is a collection and composition of those layers.

It follows then that you can minimize the total image size of your container by keeping the individual layers small, and you can minimize a layer by ensuring that each command cleans up any unnecessary data before moving to the next command.

Another technique for keeping image size down is to use multi-stage builds. Multi-stage builds are a bit too complex to describe here, but you can check out Docker's own article on it at ctohb.com/docker.

## CONTAINER ORCHESTRATION

Now that you've got reproducible images of reasonably small size managed in a hosted registry, you have to run and manage them in production. Management includes:

- Downloading and running containers on machines

- Setting up secure networking between containers/machines and other services

- Configuring service discovery/DNS

- Managing configuration and secrets for containers

- Automatically scaling services up and down with load

There are two general approaches to container management: hosted and self-managing.

## Hosted Container Management

Unless your requirements are unique or your scale is very substantial, you'll get the highest ROI from going with a hosted solution that does the bulk of the work of managing production containers for you. A common and fair criticism of these solutions is that they tend to be considerably more expensive than self-managed options and provide fewer features and more constraints. In exchange you get dramatically less overhead and less complexity, which for most startups is a tradeoff well worth making. Most small teams lack the expertise to effectively self-host, and so self-hosting ends up either requiring a substantial time investment for existing team members or forcing you to hire an expensive DevOps specialist early on. Spending an extra $1,000 a month to avoid either of those problems is likely to deliver very good ROI.

Some common hosted container platforms include Heroku, Google App Engine, Elastic Beanstalk, Google Cloud Run. Vercel is another popular hosted backend solution, though it does not run containers as described here.

## Self-Managed/Kubernetes

The most popular self-management solution for containers is called Kubernetes, often abbreviated K8s. Kubernetes is an extremely powerful and flexible, and thus complicated, system. The learning curve is steep, but the benefits and ROI are worthwhile if you're at the point of needing to self-manage your containers.

If you're considering going this route, I strongly advise against learning Kubernetes on the job. Especially for a team leader, it's too much to take on and do well on an ad-hoc basis. Instead, I recommend buying a book on Kubernetes and committing a week or two to reading it and setting up your own sandbox to get up to speed before diving in for a professional project. It's also a good idea to seek out an advisor or mentor who has a good understanding of Kubernetes to act as an accelerator for your learning of the tool.

# ClickOps vs. IaC

ClickOps refers to the process of configuring your cloud infrastructure using the user interface, as opposed to the provided APIs. As your infrastructure grows, the quantity of nuance and detail in your system will quickly exceed your ability to reproduce it with ClickOps. ClickOps is fine for prototypes or proof of concepts, but when the time comes to actually build a production environment and mirrored development environments, using ClickOps will quickly lead to considerable frustration and cost, as well as limited capability. The alternative to ClickOps is known as Infrastructure as Code (IaC).

There are several tools and frameworks that allow you to define IaC. The leading one is HashiCorp's Terraform. Terraform uses HashiCorp Config Language (HCL), a declarative configuration syntax, to allow engineers to define what resources they want and how they are to be configured. Terraform code can and should then be managed like any other code, using source control and peer review practices. Once approved, Terraform can generate infrastructure change plans and apply those plans for you with your cloud provider(s) of choice. I cannot emphasize enough how easy to use, powerful, and maintainable Terraform is, and how much ROI you're likely to gain by migrating from ClickOps to IaC.

## CONTINUOUS INTEGRATION

Continuous Integration is the process of automating the incorporation of new code into a project. That may include running static analysis on new code, running tests, building the code, and generating any required build artifacts (such as container images). Most startups use hosted CI platforms such as GitLab runners, GitHub actions, Bitbucket pipelines, Jenkins, or CircleCI to do continuous integration activities.

Some best practices for CI:

- Ensure the team understands the CI system and is comfortable adding to it, updating for new requirements, and troubleshooting when things inevitably cause the build to fail.

- Ensure builds are consistent and deterministic. Unreliable or flaky builds are an extremely powerful productivity drain and time sink.

- Try to keep build times down. For most teams a good target is for CI to take less than fifteen minutes.

- Learn the capabilities of your CI tool that aide in keeping builds fast, including build caches, build artifacts, and running jobs in parallel.

- Builds can get complex. Try to keep your code for CI *dry*. Reuse code between build pipelines where possible.

- Be consistent in how your builds access secrets. Either depend on a cloud secret manager, or build environment secrets where necessary, and try not to mix them. There should be one obvious and consistent way to handle config and secrets.

## CONTINUOUS DEPLOYMENT

In the early stages of a project, it's comparatively simple to deploy new code. At that point, there's not much code or architectural complexity. Before long, however, the need to manage dependencies, dependent services, CDNs, firewalls, build artifacts, build configuration, secrets, and more leads to a complex deploy process. As these requirements accumulate, it's easy to neglect automation, and simply rely on, for example, a dedicated and highly trusted individual as release manager. There are countless teams out there following this pattern, and I guarantee you most of those release managers have release dates circled on their calendar in advance and dread the stress, long hours, and frustration that those days inevitably entail.

Fortunately there's a cure for the error-prone stress concentration that is the monthly (or longer!) release day. It's to release every day, or heck, every hour! It follows logically from one of the Ten Pillars of Tech Culture (see page 138), "Frequency Reduces Difficulty," that more frequent releases will force your release manager, and team, to automate the hard parts of deployments. With enough iteration, releases can become entirely automated, and with sufficient testing giving you confidence in new changes, you can get to the point of triggering new releases for every code change set, referred to as "Continuous Deployment."

In addition to eliminating the complexity of the release process via automation, releasing more often means each release is of a smaller amount of code. Smaller code changes are easier for other developers to review. Smaller changes, simply by virtue of being smaller, present fewer opportunities for defects.

An automated release process tends to also imply an improved ability to roll back changes or recover from an issue in production. This is also measured as Mean Time to Recovery (MTTR).

In summary, automating releases means code goes out faster (reducing lead time), means you can deploy more often (increasing deployment frequency), and improves MTTR. That's three of the four key DORA metrics (see page 208) with one initiative!

In the companies I've worked with, either directly or in an advisory capacity, I've seen at least a dozen teams invest effort into either partially or fully moving to continuous deployment. It's not always a straightforward journey, it doesn't happen overnight, and often there are well-reasoned objections. Yet in every circumstance, when the team looks back on the time invested—be it three weeks, three months, or two years later—the difference is nothing short of transformational to the culture and overall output and velocity of the team by every metric.

## FEATURE BRANCH ENVIRONMENTS

A feature branch environment is a hosted environment and set of infrastructure that is available internally to your company, running the code from a specific branch. Feature branch environments are incredibly useful for validating that code works in a production-like setting and for enabling team members at your company to use or test changes without having to build and run code themselves. Do not underestimate human laziness; every extra step it takes somebody to test and validate your code means that they'll do the testing that much less often. Checking out code, installing dependencies, and starting servers is significantly more work than going to an automatically generated feature branch URL, and thus the feature branch will get used far more.

Feature branch environments also solve the contention problem encountered by teams that have only a single "staging" environment. I advocate giving every branch its own staging environment.

Some considerations for feature branch environments:

- Automation is key here; manually setting up feature branch environments is nearly always impractical.

- Where possible, use a system such as Vercel or Firebase that includes feature branch environments as a first-class feature to minimize your setup and maintenance costs.

- Carefully consider how to treat data in feature branch environments. You'll need to answer the following questions:

  ○ Does each backend feature branch environment get a new database? My recommendation is yes.

  ○ Does the feature branch environment use production data? My recommendation is no. Instead, use a seed script that generates similar quantities of data to production. It is worthwhile to have a process that copies, sanitizes, and restores production data for developers when necessary for debugging.

  ○ How are database schema changes/migrations handled in feature branch environments?

  ○ How does service discovery work in feature branch environments for service-oriented architectures? Often you can get away with having a common set of services and deploy feature branch versions of just the service under test. I recommend that you have an environment for every service that is always running called integration. Have all feature branches reference the integration environment of other services. Each integration environment update should be a production update, but you should also allow developers to deploy feature branch code temporarily to integration environments for cross-service integration testing.

Having looked at this list of concerns, you may be daunted by the burden of setting up and maintaining feature branches. Indeed, a proper feature branch setup is not cheap, but the value it offers is substantial in improving your ability to test, and in reducing the logistical overhead required to verify different kinds of software changes.

## MANAGING DNS

Knowing how the domain name system (DNS) works, and knowing how to manage DNS and its security implications for your company, is a critical job that often lands on the startup CTO. If you're not already familiar with the basics of how DNS works and the different record types, I recommend you spend a few minutes browsing Wikipedia now to get a grounding on the subject.

You should also know how DNS is used for email in your organization. In particular, become familiar with Sender Policy Framework (SPF) records and DKIM/DMARC.

You should also set up your DNS records using Infrastructure as Code (IaC). I've seen countless companies where DNS is managed exclusively by an executive whose two-factor authentication is the only one allowed to update a zone record, and when that person is on vacation there's no fall-back mechanism to manage the site.

A better solution is to set up DNS with Terraform (which has integrations with all the major DNS providers) and then manage DNS records with source control, empowering individual developers to add new records in a responsible way that isn't gated on any one individual.

### Decoupling Shipping Code from Shipping Features (Feature Toggles)

At a high level, a feature toggle is a switch that allows you to change system behavior without changing the actual code. I strongly advocate using feature toggles, in particular because they allow your team to have separate processes and timelines for shipping code and shipping features. Pete Hodgson has a wonderful, in-depth explanation of feature toggles at ctohb.com/hodgson.

The Four Key Metrics advocate for shipping code as frequently as possible. Doing so leads to many great positive benefits for the health of your engineering process. A natural concern, however, is that your business may not be ready for a particular feature to go live the second the code is done. There are many reasons why your development and release schedules might be out of sync in this way, such as the need to coordinate timing with a marketing activation, the creation of customer support documentation, awaiting regulatory approvals, pausing for internal communication, etc. Feature toggles enable your engineering team to focus on shipping as quickly and reliably as possible and delegate the problem of coordinating when features are enabled to an out-of-band process likely owned by other teams.

## SYSTEM MONITORING: APMS AND RUMS

Application performance monitoring (APM) and real user monitoring (RUM) are two types of tools that help teams understand how an application is performing in production and identify or prevent user-facing outages.

An APM tool usually sits inside or alongside your application in the production environment and provides analytics and insights into resource usage and request latency and throughput from the perspective of your backend. RUM is an external tool that pretends to be a user and provides analytics on latency from the frontend's perspective, or the perspective of a "real user."

If you had to choose one (and these tools are often very expensive, so you may be forced to go with one or the other), choose the one that covers the blind spot more likely to be problematic for your application. If you have tons of users and you get inundated with real-time complaints for every minor bug or edge case, then an APM monitoring backend load may prove more valuable than a RUM producing redundant alerts to your users. For most startups in seed or growth stages, though, you'll likely have inconsistent application usage, especially covering your edge cases, in which case RUM may be more valuable than an APM on a mostly idle backend.

Some common tools in this space are New Relic, Datadog, and Akamai mPulse.

# 3.4 Testing

Imagine that, instead of testing software code, your job was to be the inspector for a municipal bridge. The bridge is built and now it's your job to inspect it and decide whether or not to allow it to open to the public. Do you inspect every single bolt and rivet on the bridge? Doing so would probably give you high confidence the bridge was safe, but it would also take a long time and derail the mayor's plans to open the bridge next week.

Another reasonable strategy would be to decide exactly which elements of the bridge are essential to meet the designated safety factor and test/inspect those. Maybe that's only every other rivet, plus all the cables and structural concrete.

Similarly, in software engineering testing, the goal isn't coverage for coverage's sake, but coverage that provides confidence that the software does what it is intended to do.

Effective software testing is not always about 100 percent code coverage. The bar for a good software test suite is that it gives your team confidence that, when the build is green and all tests pass, the software is ready to be released to end users. That may mean 100 percent code coverage, or it may mean 30 percent code coverage. The exact number is up to you to determine and monitor, and that amount of effort may change over time if you find the tests aren't providing the same confidence they once were (and, conversely, if you find you're overinvesting—i.e., you're spending a lot of resources on a test suite, yet bugs are still making it out too often).

## TESTING/QUALITY ASSURANCE TEAMS

Depending on the size of your team, you'll either have no dedicated test team, one test team working on one or many types of tests, or many test teams working on various kinds of software testing. No matter who is doing the test it's important to recognize that software testing is a complicated process, and nuance matters. To test software effectively, the tester, whether they wrote the code or it was thrown over the fence to them, has to deeply understand what the code/software should be doing. Your role is to set up your teams so that they can empathize with each other. To do this, ensure that the teams share goals/KPIs, that your process has robust and continuous communication between the developer and tester, and monitor that the teams have a healthy, productive relationship.

## TEST QUALITY

Before jumping into the nuts and bolts of the different software testing paradigms, it's worth thinking about what the purpose of software testing is, and thus what makes a good test, and conversely what makes a bad test.

Defining bad tests is simple. Bad tests have a higher cost than benefit to your team. Some common characteristics of bad tests:

- It takes more time to maintain and fix tests for legitimate code changes than the pain you save by bugs found.

- The test has a high false positive rate or is inconsistent, which slows down CI and causes developers frustration and context-switching cost to re-run spurious failures.

- The test is poorly thought out and literally validates that the code does the wrong thing.

- The suite tests that the code does the right thing and has low false positives, but it's so convoluted and hard to understand that only the person who wrote the test can add a new one, and every other engineer who looks at it gets a migraine.

- The test does not instill confidence that the code under evaluation is ready to be shipped to end users.

With that picture in mind, it's relatively easy to see by contrast what attributes good tests should have. Good tests are:

- Easy and fast to run both locally and in a shared CI environment

- Capable of running reliably and consistently producing the same result

- Easy to augment

- Easy to refactor or update for underlying logical changes

- Appropriately coupled to the underlying code patterns, testing at the right "altitude" (so to speak) to capture breakages that matter

- Easy for any engineer to understand and work on

One of the best ways to evaluate your testing approach is also the most obvious: ask how your team feels about the tests with a simple sentiment analysis. The results tend to be very binary—either tests are a source of security that teams rely on, and naturally augment them because they obviously are a net value-add; or teams passively, or even actively, hate their tests because they're a drain on productivity with not enough obvious value.

## WHAT TO TEST

Your team should be adding testing in ways that boost confidence that the system works correctly while minimizing the additional burden of maintaining those tests long term in the face of organic system growth. A general pattern to minimize this pain is to test the public interface. Public interfaces should be well thought out and comparably stable over time. They are also the happy path that consumers of the software will actually experience.

Tests on public interfaces should therefore change little over time and also provide confidence that the parts of the code that matter are working correctly.

The public interface for your software may vary from project to project. For many projects, it'll be an actual HTTP-based API; for some, it'll be a set of functions/classes in a library or internal service. For other projects it may be a user interface.

## TESTING TYPE COMPARISON

Software testing can be broken down into the following categories/paradigms:

- Unit testing

- Integration testing

- End-to-end testing

- Manual testing

- Semi-automated testing

The attributes that differentiate these types of testing are as follows:

- **Code planning:** How much forethought is required in the actual writing of the code to ensure it's testable under this test paradigm.

- **Test scope:** How much each test can evaluate at once.

- **Change granularity detection:** What size of, or type of, code change a test is likely to detect and cause a failure.

- **Run cost:** How quickly or how costly it is to run the tests, in time or in dollars.

- **Addition effort:** How much effort is required to add additional coverage.

- **Setup effort:** How much effort is necessary to set up an effective test suite.

The following chart summarizes how the five paradigms map to these metrics. Note that there is no one perfect test paradigm; each has tradeoffs, and I encourage you to think carefully about which tradeoffs make sense for your company and codebase. The right answer is usually a blend of different test paradigms, using each type of test where it adds the most value in your application.

## TABLE: 5 TESTING TYPE PARADIGMS

| | Code Planning/ Forethought | Test Scope | Change Granularity Detection | Run Cost | Addition Effort | Setup Effort |
|---|---|---|---|---|---|---|
| Unit Tests | High | Very Small | Very Small | Low | Low | Low |
| Integration Tests | Medium | Medium | Medium | Medium | Medium/ Low | Medium/ Low |
| End-to-End Tests | Low | High | High | Medium/ High | Medium | Medium/ High |
| Manual Testing | None | High | Depends | Very High | Low | Low |
| Semi-Automated Testing | None | High | Depends | Medium | Medium/ Low | Medium |

## UNIT TESTS

Unit testing is often the first thing that comes to mind when somebody talks about software testing. It's widely what's taught in school and included in textbooks, and it usually gets the most effort in the real world. Given all this, you'd think unit tests were the best type of test, though I'd argue that's not always the case. Let's begin by clearly defining unit tests so as to differentiate them from other testing paradigms.

Unit tests run entirely in memory on a machine, in a shared memory space with the code under evaluation, without requiring any network connectivity or dependency on external services. Most unit tests are very fast to run, test very small amounts of code at a time, and are relatively easy to get started with. Unit tests are usually also tightly coupled to your code contracts and often require new code in the form of mocks to enable code-under-test to execute without normally available external dependencies.

The key tradeoff made by unit tests—and their primary downside—is that they are tightly coupled to the code under test. It's altogether too easy to have unit tests be deeply intertwined with actual function calls and internal data objects. This deep dependency means any refactor of the code—even simple and benign changes—will require considerable unit test updates as well. The creation of mocks and test data fixtures often also requires a considerable amount of code to create and maintain to allow unit tests to run, adding unexpected cost to the unit testing framework.

## INTEGRATION TESTS

An integration test relaxes the in-memory and zero-dependency constraints of unit tests. As a result, integration tests tend to run slower and integrate with code-under-test at a higher level. When they run in a different process from code under test, they're usually exercising an externally exposed contract, such as an API. This means that internal refactors that don't change API behavior tend to go unnoticed by an integration test, making these tests overall less brittle but also less likely to detect smaller side effects.

In addition, integration tests require the creation of fewer or no mocks and, as a result, can be less code to implement.

## END-TO-END TESTS

An end-to-end (e2e) test exercises code in the same manner as the end user. For backend code, end-to-end tests and integration tests may function in the same way, running code via an external contract. For user-facing frontend code, an end-to-end test usually involves mechanizing the client interface, often a web browser or mobile phone. I would not encourage any tech leader to write their own client mechanizing code—this is a particularly gnarly problem that downloadable tools like Selenium, Cypress, and Puppeteer can take off your hands. For mobile, there are tools like HeadSpin and Detox.

The key tradeoff of end-to-end tests, in the real world, is reliability. At least at the time of writing, reliable web end-to-end tests are still somewhat elusive; the nature of how the browser renders means race conditions occur very easily by accident. Building a reliable web end-to-end test suite requires considerable care, attention to detail, and maintenance.

The payoff, though, is not insubstantial, as it's possible to create very high test coverage and very high confidence in functionality of user-facing flows with e2e test suites. There are several companies, including testim.io and rainforestqa.com, that are exploring using AI and ML to solve this problem. These solutions deploy fuzzy "visual" testing instead of relying on the presence or absence of CSS selectors, for example, to try and improve test reliability. Hopefully by the time you read this, the state of the art will have advanced a bit further, and the value proposition of end-to-end tests will be even stronger than at the time of this writing.

## VISUAL REGRESSION TESTING

Visual regression testing is a relatively new paradigm that aims to detect defects in user-facing applications by performing deltas on rendered visuals. There are frameworks that do that at various levels of granularity, ranging from capturing screenshots of entire pages to rendering individual components, and producing deltas to detect defects. The obvious drawback is that every intentional change to any visual tested component will require a change to a test.

Fortunately, these test frameworks often make it simple and painless to reproduce the set of "correct" visuals for comparison, which opens up another pitfall: with easy tooling to overwrite the testing target, it becomes very easy to produce false negatives, accidentally accepting a visual delta that is, in fact, erroneous.

## MANUAL TESTING

Manual testing, as the name implies, is run by humans and not machine code. For humans testing code, we can further subdivide this category into specialized and unspecialized testers.

### SPECIALIZED MANUAL TESTING

Specialized manual testing is an in-house manual testing team. Beyond the traditional benefits of an in-house team, such as aligned incentives and a long-term working relationship, the value of being in-house is that the team can build expertise in your product and deeply understand your users. This allows the team to identify defects that an untrained or unfamiliar tester would miss. A high-quality testing team can not only serve as a resource for catching software defects but also contribute valuable feedback on a product level, identifying inconsistencies in design, and asking provocative questions about how or why something works the way it does. A great in-house manual testing team can provide a huge improvement in overall software and product quality.

Specialized manual testing teams should be creating detailed test plans for product functionality and storing those plans in an easy-to-retrieve/repeat fashion, ideally with a tool like TestRail that allows creating full test suites of manual test plans which can be rerun by the team manually on demand. Another benefit of a tool like this is integration with other developer and product tools—for example, linking a TestRail run to a Jira epic to show how many manual and regression tests were run for the release of a given feature. Not only is this valuable as a launch checklist item, but it also aids in retrospectives for any released defects, allowing you to revisit what manual tests were run before releasing any given feature, and adding additional manual tests to catch any defects that made it through.

## UNSPECIALIZED MANUAL TESTING

Unspecialized manual testing is often referred to as crowdsourced testing. There are several proprietary platforms for sourcing testers, such as Rainforest QA, Pay4Bugs, 99Tests, and Testlio. The pricing model for these platforms usually varies based on the number of validated bugs submitted. Depending on the nature of your product and the types of defects you're looking to optimize for, crowdsourced testing can be a very cost-effective and low-effort way to improve product quality.

## SEMI-AUTOMATED TESTING

Semi-automated testing is a relatively new category of software testing. These tests are created by non-technical staff—perhaps your specialized manual testing team—and then run in either a completely automated or supervised environment.

The major pitfall of these tests is reliability. Because they're created by non-technical staff, they may not be quite as precise as fully automated tests, making them more prone to false positives and false negatives. That said, this space is rapidly evolving with new companies and tools launching every year, such as Rainforest QA and Testim, with strategies to improve reliability and lower overall cost.

# 3.5 Source Control

The industry standard used by the vast majority of companies for managing source control is Git. There would need to be a very compelling reason for your organization to use anything else; most of your current and future team members will arrive already knowing the basics of Git. By not using it, you'd likely be inflicting an unnecessary learning curve on them by forcing them to learn your chosen alternative.

There are three main cloud Git hosting platforms: GitLab, GitHub, and Bitbucket. These three have the lion's share of the market and, again, you should think carefully before deviating from these standards.

Git has an interestingly shaped learning curve. Most people reach a plateau where they operate with a rudimentary understanding that gets them by for most happy path testing scenarios. However, sometimes things go wrong, and a developer loses a commit or makes a mess with a merge. When this happens, their failure to climb the rest of the Git learning curve will cause frustration and slowdown. I encourage you, as the team lead, to invest the effort to climb the back half of the curve. Use Git exclusively on the command line to become familiar with what is actually happening. Learn about the reflog, interactive rebases, bisect, and the various built-in merge strategies. Armed with this knowledge, you can bypass an entire class of productivity-draining problems and train your team to become Git experts as well.

## PEER REVIEW

In general, experts recommend implementing a robust peer review process for all code changes. (As I write this in early 2023, there is a growing movement challenging this recommendation, or at the least adding nuance to it, which I'll discuss in the next section.) Most peer review is done with what is called—depending on your code hosting solution—a pull request, code review, or merge request. Here are some suggestions for keeping code review productive and efficient:

- Keep reviews small! Set a maximum size for code reviews, something like ten files and 200 lines. Anything else should be broken out into multiple stacked/incremental reviews. (A stacked review is a code review that is based on or dependent on a prior review. When completed, the reviews are merged sequentially to add up to a complete change.)

- Establish the goals for code review upfront with your team and bake them into your culture. Code review is not for style or petty semantics; that's what your auto code formatter/linter and static analysis are for. Code review's purpose is to ensure clarity, identify architectural concerns, flag defects and deviations from patterns, note edge cases, and guarantee adherence to business rules.

- Require the author to make the reviewer's job easy. Authors should include a description of the change, a link to relevant requirements and tickets, and a video walkthrough (using a tool like loom.com) of the code and the code working as intended.

- Encourage the author of any given code review to do a self-review before asking others to review. A few well-placed comments from the author to guide readers can save a lot of time.

- Set aside dedicated review times/windows to minimize disruptions.

## SHIP, SHOW, ASK

The common wisdom is that every code change should be reviewed by two people before being shipped to customers. As with everything, there are tradeoffs. Manual code review is not free, nor is it a guarantee of software quality. Given that manual code review comes at a cost, it's worth thinking about when that cost provides the highest return and using code review as a tool for the highest-ROI scenarios. This general idea was popularized by a 2021 blog post by Rouan Wilsenach titled "Ship/Show/Ask" (ctohb.com/ssa).

Let's examine the cost of code review. A code review requires two people—call them the Author and the Reviewer—to experience a number of context switches. A common asynchronous code pattern might be as follows:

- **Context Switch #1:** Author stops coding on Project 1, sets up code review, and tags Reviewer. Author starts working on Project 2.

- **Context Switch #2:** Reviewer gets a notification, stops their work on Project 3, and begins review of Project 1. Reviewer leaves feedback for Author, resumes work on Project 3.

- **Context Switch #3:** Author is notified of feedback on Project 1, stops work on Project 2, and addresses comments from Reviewer. Then Author resumes work on Project 2.

- **Context Switch #4:** Reviewer stops work on Project 3 and—best-case scenario—Reviewer is now satisfied with changes in Project 1 and approves the code review. Reviewer resumes work on Project 3. Worst case, Author and Reviewer must repeat Context Switches #3 and #4 several times.

- **Context Switch #5:** Author is notified of approval, stops work on Project 2, merges Project 1, then resumes work on Project 2.

There are ways to minimize these context switches, but they too involve tradeoffs. A common alternative is to do all code reviews as a synchronous "pair programming" exercise; however, that strategy trades context switches for synchronous meeting time, which is still a drag on productivity. No matter how you slice it, human code review is expensive.

My suggested alternative is to classify types of work by their level of risk, and the expected benefit from code reviews. A sample classification system:

- Trivial changes—no approval required
  - Copy/translation updates
  - Minor UI changes, ideally submitted with visual evidence of the change
  - Test-only changes
  - New code that is explicitly not yet used or is disabled behind a feature toggle
  - Code that no customer or user is able to access (e.g., hidden pages)
- Minor changes—minimal review or after-the-fact review
  - Code changes that come with tests and involve augmentation of existing patterns and functionality
  - Code that has limited or no real-world usage (e.g., an undeployed product)
  - Refactors that can be proven are correct via reliable testing
- Major changes—careful upfront review
  - Anything involving new tools, frameworks, patterns, or architecture
  - Significant new features
  - Anything involving sensitive data or PII or with potential impact on security posture

Although I believe this system improves overall team efficiency, I concede that it's not an option for everyone. Many compliance regimes (such as PCI or SOC 2) require a policy of 100 percent human code review. The best you can do in that scenario is comply and perhaps carve out products or feature areas that are not governed by the compliance framework to experiment with a more nuanced and efficient process.

## BRANCHING MODELS

There are many ways to deal with source control branching, though the industry as a whole is building momentum around the concept of trunk-based development. As this seems to be the most effective and commonly used pattern at this time, it's what we'll discuss here. If you're seriously considering a different pattern, you'll find plentiful resources online discussing methodologies and best practices for alternative approaches.

There are many blog posts with helpful graphics covering git branching models, such as this one from Reviewpad: ctohb.com/branching. If the following description doesn't make sense to you, I urge you to consult any of these posts and their associated visuals.

In a traditional branching model—sometimes referred to as "GitFlow"—there are two long-lived branches, a "main" and a "develop" branch. Work is done based on develop in feature branches and then is often forked to another release branch for any given release, and then finally back merged to main. Hotfixes are then done off of main while further development is done off of develop. This system involves no less than four branches for every change to get to production, and involves maintaining many branches simultaneously. For these reasons and others, GitFlow has largely fallen out of favor and is no longer considered best practice.

Trunk-based development, and its slightly more sophisticated cousin, GitHub Flow, are models of managing source code that aim to minimize the number and duration of branches. The exact implementation of GitHub Flow and trunk-based development will vary, but what they have in common is that there is a single branch whose name varies and doesn't matter much. Here we'll call it "production." Production is always deployable. In fact, I recommend that you set up automation so every commit to production can actually be deployed to production. Work can then be done in feature branches off of production, reviewed in the feature branch, and merged when ready. That's it—one long-lived branch and many short-lived (and ideally small) feature branches.

For this model to work well, you need a handful of prerequisites:

- Continuous Integration that runs a robust test suite to ensure that feature branches are safe to merge.

- A culture and an implementation of using feature toggles so branches can be merged quickly and then features deployed/enabled at a later date when it makes sense for the business.

- Robust monitoring of production to detect changes.

- The ability to rapidly deploy, with zero downtime, code changes to the production environment. Similarly, an ability to rapidly revert individual changes in response to an incident.

- A culture that is disciplined about small and short-lived feature branches. The GitHub Flow model loses its efficiency and simplicity if feature branches become large, long-lived and unwieldy. As discussed in the 3.3.5 Feature Branch Environments, small commits, small branches. and small pull requests are a key driver of productivity.

## LONG-LIVED VS. SHORT-LIVED BRANCHES

The key to maintaining a smooth system of branches and merges with your team is to keep branches short-lived. Nearly all of the problems associated with code merging come from code branches being open too long or the branch containing too large a diff (ctohb.com/diffs). In general, a short-lived branch should be open just a few days, or two weeks at the absolute most.

Keep in mind that a feature doesn't necessarily have to be implemented in a single branch. For example, you can have an initial branch with just tests that is reviewed and merged, and then followed up by a branch with the implementation. Alternatively, you can build an implementation that isn't connected to the main application, have it reviewed and merged, then build the connection and tests in a subsequent branch.

With a bit of thought and practice most implementations can be broken down into independently mergeable pieces. This is a skill that—with your guidance—teams can develop over time.

Benefits of keeping branches short-lived:

- Limits the amount of time for new code from other branches to be merged into trunk, thus limiting the scope for code conflicts. Smaller branches also inherently have less surface area for conflicts.

- Keeps the feature branch code relatively small, thus making it easier for reviewers to read and limiting the scope for breakages.

- Encourages faster feedback in reviews, and allows for course corrections sooner in the process of implementing features.

- Encourages your team to have a reliable Continuous Integration system. Frequent merges will highlight deficiencies in your build/test environment, making it painful if the systems are unreliable and motivating improvements to those systems.

# 3.6 Production Escalations

An escalator is a tool that takes in incidents and manages an on-call rotation, paging the on-call engineer and then escalating to others if pages go unacknowledged. PagerDuty is likely the most popular of these tools.

## IMPLEMENTING ESCALATORS

Before you implement an escalator and set up a rotation, make sure the engineers on your team have opted in to being on rotation, and that everyone knows and understands expectations for creating exceptions (e.g., trading an on-call window with somebody else during a vacation).

You'll also want to ensure that you have adequate documentation in place, and that everyone understands the standard procedures for what to do when receiving a page. Some considerations for establishing these procedures:

- Note where the recipient should post an acknowledgment of receipt of the page (maybe in the escalator tool itself or a shared group chat dedicated specifically to handling escalations).

- Enable easy access to the playbooks that are used to help diagnose particular kinds of problems.

- Determine whether to, and where to, set up any kind of "site down" notice (e.g., a company status page needs updating).

- Decide where and how often to post updates on the status of the investigation, impact estimate, and restoration estimate.

- Determine what to do once an incident is closed, scheduling a root cause analysis exercise and ensuring the particular incident does not recur.

## ROOT CAUSE ANALYSIS (RCA) EXERCISES

Any time there is a system issue that has measurable user impact, your team should perform some level of root cause analysis (RCA). The goal of an RCA is to understand where your systems had a failure that allowed an impactful defect to make it to production and to end users.

To be crystal clear, the root cause analysis *must not* be about identifying fault or assigning blame. That needs to be true in every part of the RCA process and embedded into the culture of your team. The RCA attacks systemic problems (not human errors) in your system that allow a failure to occur.

Without that safety and willingness for team members to be forthright with their feedback and documentation, you'll miss out on key opportunities to improve the system.

## RCA DOCUMENTS

Your team should produce documentation in some form for every RCA. Depending on how often issues occur with your system, and the nature of those issues, you may wish to create a classification system for RCAs, with low-impact incidents getting a lighter-weight RCA process than high-impact incidents. It should be acknowledged that a thorough RCA on a high-impact incident is an expensive effort, taking considerable time and thoughtfulness, and that it may prove too heavy-handed for trivial defects.

That said, for most companies it's better to err on the side of overspending in this area and ensuring greater reliability. You should start with a thorough RCA on everything, and transition to a stratified RCA system once you've got a good understanding of the landscape and impact of the kinds of issues your team will face.

For issues that merit a full, thoughtful analysis, here is a template that will get you started and asking your team the right questions: ctohb.com/ rca. It is a good practice—and in fact a requirement for most compliance frameworks—to create a new document like this for every incident and to organize them in an internal company document store for later reference.

## RCA MEETINGS AND TIMELINE

As soon as it is practical after you've resolved an incident, designate an appropriate person to serve as the lead on an RCA. The lead should clone the template and begin filling in relevant data about the incident and beginning to explore the Five Whys (ctohb.com/5whys) for the incident. They should complete an initial draft of the RCA and circulate it to relevant peers before scheduling a time as a group to explore and try and improve the analysis and future prevention steps.

The meeting attendees should read the RCA draft in advance and come prepared to explore the nuts and bolts of the incident and ideate on future prevention steps.

### Choosing the RCA Lead Author

The RCA lead need not necessarily be the person who responded to the incident. The ideal RCA lead should be someone who is very familiar with the systems involved and can ask insightful questions about where tools and processes failed and generate ideas for improvement.

Note that we're not throwing anyone who made a human error under the bus. That person may be the RCA lead if they fit the prior criteria, but their error does not on its own make them the right person to lead the RCA. They should certainly contribute and take the opportunity to learn through the process. But again, they are not punished for their mistake as part of the process. Authoring an RCA is not a punishment; it's an important responsibility and element of system maintenance.

### Scheduling RCA Remediation Work

A good RCA process will often identify many work items for the team to improve the system and make future incidents less likely. The natural next question is: do we do them now? For the engineers involved, the answer is likely yes; for a manager concerned about hitting deadlines and a road-map, the answer will be less clear.

There is no one right answer to the question, but here is some general guidance:

- Never let a good crisis go to waste. Motivation to remediate issues will be at its peak around the incident and the RCA meeting, and highly motivated engineers are often most efficient. It's also easy to underesti-mate the overall cost to your team of system reliability issues and thus under prioritize reliability improvements. The fact that a production incident occurred should remind you and your team that these invest-ments are critical to limiting distractions and enabling teams to focus on productive feature work and delivering consistent high velocity.

- The level of effort for many remedial issues is likely to vary widely. Some typical tickets might be "add more logging" or "change a setting in our CI provider to ensure PRs with failing builds cannot be merged." These types of trivial tickets cost more to maintain and groom in a backlog than they'd take just to do in the moment, so just do them. The chances they are the wrong thing to do are pretty low, and if negative conse-quences result, they can be easily reversed.

- For high-effort remediation steps, I encourage you to triage those and put them through your regular planning process. Often, high-effort remediation steps can be simplified with the benefit of time and plan-ning. Said another way, the identified right way to solve the problem on day one may not be the ideal solution, and only by putting the issue through the regular paces of technical scrutiny can a better, perhaps less costly, solution emerge.

# 3.7 IT

Here I refer to IT, information technology, as internal company tooling and technology used to conduct business on a daily basis. This is in contrast to the technology your company is building for its customer product. IT usually comprises tools like company hardware (desktops, laptops, and phones), VPNs, email, antivirus and monitoring software, etc. As a startup in the modern world, whether you're an in-person or remote team, if you make a few wise decisions, you should not need to spend very much time or capital on IT.

Some key decisions that will help you minimize IT cost at most small tech companies:

- Use a cloud-based system for company email, data, and documents. Most startups are using Google Workspace, but if your team members (and prospective future hires) are more comfortable with an alternative, go with that. There's no benefit at this stage in setting up your own in-house mail server, document storage, data access, networking, etc.

- Early on, unless required to by a compliance system, don't require employees to use company hardware. At small scale purchasing (especially pre-product market fit), provisioning and managing company hardware is a non-trivial effort (and cost!) that provides only marginal or rare real-world benefits.

- It's perhaps painful to acknowledge, but properly securing your product and IT system is a considerable task, and unrealistic for a young startup to do exhaustively early on. I encourage you to be pragmatic and focus on securing your system from the most likely sources of breach or data theft: human error by your employees. It's far more likely your engineering team forgot to put authentication in front of an API, or somebody leaves their laptop unlocked at a coffee shop, than an attacker manages to man in the middle your data or hack into your cloud infrastructure using an exploit.

Even following best practices to minimize IT effort, you'll still have some IT tasks you cannot avoid, primarily around activating and deactivating user accounts and password recovery for employees. I encourage you to document for and train other coworkers, perhaps in HR, in how to do these tasks so they do not interrupt you or the engineering team on a regular basis.

# 3.8 Security and Compliance

In this section, I will provide a brief overview of the subject of security and compliance for startups. You can and should put in the effort to find in-depth resources beyond this book on these topics.

## AUTH SECURITY TERMINOLOGY

Especially with security, it's important to be precise and exact with language. Some definitions of commonly misused terms:

- **Authentication, or AuthN**: Validating that a user or client is who they say they are. Your login system performs user authentication.

- **Authorization, or AuthZ**: Validating that a user or client has permission to do what they're trying to do. Your role-based access control (RBAC) or permission system does authorization.

- **2FA or MFA**: Two-factor authentication and multi-factor authentication is the process of authenticating with a service using more than one type of credential. This is typically done with a password (first factor) and some kind of proof-of-ownership, e.g., an emailed one-time password (proving you own the email), SMS (proving you own a phone number), or timed one-time-password (TOPT) (proving you own a device/passkey). Note that due to the prevalence of SIM Porting attacks, where an attacker has the ability to intercept or reroute SMS, using SMS as a second factor is generally discouraged.

## SECURITY AT STARTUPS

Startups are often defined by the extent to which they are resource-constrained. As a result, security posture and compliance are often the first things deprioritized on the to-do list, as they are less likely to represent an existential threat to the business than other pressing concerns. If you have no users or revenue, what is there for a hacker to steal?

Taking security into account can also become a drag on productivity or an expensive task, especially if your mission is to secure a system that already exists. But if you're starting from day one, you have the opportunity to make good decisions at the start that create a strong security posture with minimal additional cost.

Some ways to incorporate security at your startup that won't cost you much:

- Establish security as a priority in the mindset of your team in your onboarding and training materials.

- Enroll all engineers in onboarding and recurring basic security training—things like the OWASP Top Ten or various gamified security training that take a few minutes a month to keep security top of mind.

- Rely on proven and well-maintained tools for anything related to authentication or authorization.

- Don't waste time building a login page yourself; in 2023 there's really no reason to. Tools like Auth0, SuperTokens, and AWS Cognito provide secure user signup, login, social login, forgotten password management, email authentication, two-factor authentication, and session management. Some of these tools also offer robust authorization systems. Dealing with auth is a substantial project; it's very complex and mistakes are expensive. There's no reason your startup needs to solve that problem.

- Don't be lazy about IT security. Regardless of whether you're using Dropbox, Box, Google Drive, SharePoint, etc., take a few minutes and set policies to help avoid human error, such as default sharing permissions to being internal only. Set up regular data-sharing reports and appoint an employee to do a quarterly audit of permissions settings on any particularly sensitive documents or spreadsheets.

- Use an enterprise password management solution, such as 1Password, and ensure all employees are using robust passwords for important tools. Similarly, use Single Sign-On (SSO) as often as possible and ensure your SSO provider is configured with high security (at least requiring Multi-Factor Authentication).

- Don't commit secrets in your codebase. Leverage a secure secret manager such as Google Cloud Secret Manager or AWS Secret Manager, and commit the name/location of a secret in code and resolve that name to a value in production, either at bootup time using a tool like Berglas or Whisper, or at runtime directly with the secret manager APIs.

## COMPLIANCE

Whether it's due to the industry you are in, the size of your business, or the nature of your customers, most startups need to comply with at least one formal compliance framework. If your users are in Europe, then you need to comply with GDPR. If you're taking in user data, it's wise to understand the CCPA. If you're working with enterprise clients, you'll be asked for your SOC 2 or ISO 27001 certification. In healthcare, you've got HIPAA, and if you're in payments, you've likely heard of PCI DSS.

For a startup, staying in compliance with any or all of these frameworks can be unacceptably expensive. Here are some tips for staying compliant and anticipating the cost:

- Don't try to get a compliance certificate at the last minute. Preparing for and conducting an audit such as for PCI DSS or SOC 2 from start to finish is a lengthy process, ranging from six to twelve months for most startups. Starting early and maintaining compliance is cheaper than starting late and doing rework.

- Use as much automation to enforce or provide evidence of compliance as possible. There is a thriving sector of SaaS companies who specialize in automating these compliance frameworks; companies like Vanta, Tugboat Logic, Secureframe, Laika, and Drata all have offerings that will reduce your time-to-certification and total cost significantly.

- If you're lucky enough to have a formal compliance person or department, lean into that relationship. The more proactive you can be in sharing plans with a compliance department, and the earlier you incorporate their feedback, the less costly and frustrating staying compliant will be.

# 4

# CONCLUSION: MEASURING SUCCESS

You've put together a great hiring process, the team is happy, you're running sprints like a pro, and your architecture is withstanding the growing demands of the business. That feels good, but how do you know if it's enough? How do we measure our own success and performance as a technical leader or CTO?

One way to look at defining greatness in this role might be from a CFO's perspective: how efficiently can a CTO deploy an R&D budget and convert that into engineering and product output?

Or perhaps one might look at it from the CEO's viewpoint: how quickly can the team the CTO leads deliver on certain business objectives?

Or, given how important people leadership is to excelling in this role, we could view it through a humanistic lens: is your team doing their best work? After all, a great CTO's mission is to build an organizational culture that allows individual engineers to do their best work and achieve the impossible with technology.

Or, rather than trying to define a single objective, maybe the best definition of CTO greatness is a sum of all the skills that a CTO might exercise on a daily basis. Perhaps "great" is when you take the sum of architecture, performance management, vendor management, executive leadership, cultural contributions, public evangelism, mentorship, and DevOps, put it through a formula, and you end up with a number bigger than 42.

CONCLUSION: MEASURING SUCCESS

Try as we might, it seems that great leadership—even great *technical* leadership—isn't something we can precisely quantify or measure. Smart minds will struggle to agree on a common description of greatness, but we will all agree that the role is diverse and ever-changing, requiring constant learning and adaptation.

There are few universal truths in engineering leadership, but one of them is that becoming a good engineering leader is a never-ending journey of self-improvement, discovery, and growth. Proceeding down this path requires humility, willingness to make mistakes, and, above all, curiosity and a desire to learn.

I hope this handbook has been a helpful reference guide for you with the challenges you face on your leadership journey. The handbook covers many of the challenges that I myself have faced over the years as well as those of the many wonderful leaders I've had the pleasure of interacting with. I've done my best to provide some structure on meeting those challenges, though every situation is unique, and ultimately the path you take is yours to devise and the results are yours to own.

At some point in life, one gets asked: "What advice would you give to the younger version of yourself?" This handbook is my answer to that question. I hope it helps you in your journey to build powerful technology, motivated and empowered teams, and successful businesses, and, most of all, have fun and do some good for the world.

# 5

# BOOK REFERENCES

- *Getting Things Done* by David Allen

- *Extreme Programming Explained* by Kent Beck

- *Work Rules!* by Laszlo Bock

- *How to Win Friends and Influence People* by Dale Carnegie

- *Agile Estimating and Planning* by Mike Cohn

- *Good to Great* by Jim Collins

- *The 7 Habits of Highly Effective People* by Stephen Covey

- *Domain-Driven Design* by Eric Evans

- *Patterns of Enterprise Application Architecture* by Martin Fowler

- *High Output Management* by Andy Grove

- *Scaling Up* by Verne Harnish

- *The Hard Thing About Hard Things* by Ben Horowitz

- *Immunity to Change* by Robert Kegan

- *The Phoenix Project* by Gene Kim

- *The Five Dysfunctions of a Team* by Patrick Lencioni

- *Managing Humans* by Michael Lopp

BOOK REFERENCES

- *Team of Teams* by Stanley McChrystal
- *Escaping the Build Trap* by Melissa Perri
- *Good Authority* by Jonathan Raymond
- *Good Strategy/Bad Strategy* by Richard Rumelt
- *Radical Candor* by Kim Scott
- *The Art of Agile Development* by James Shore and Shane Warden
- *Scrum: The Art of Doing Twice the Work in Half the Time* by Jeff Sutherland
- *Extreme Ownership* by Jocko Willink and Leif Babin

# DIGITAL REFERENCES

- **VSCode's Setting Files** (ctohb.com/vscode): https://code.visualstudio.com/docs/getstarted/settings
- **Key to Gmail** (ctohb.com/keytogmail): https://techcrunch.com/2010/03/14/key-to-gmail
- **Shit Umbrella** (ctohb.com/umbrella): https://medium.com/@rajsarkar/word-of-the-month-shit-umbrella-33e3182a0f1b
- **Liar's Paradox** (ctohb.com/liarsparadox): https://en.wikipedia.org/wiki/Liar_paradox
- **Gitlab Compensation Calculator** (ctohb.com/gitlabcompcalc): https://about.gitlab.com/handbook/total-rewards/compensation/
- **Five Whys** (ctohb.com/5whys): https://en.wikipedia.org/wiki/Five_whys
- **Take the DORA DevOps Quick Check** (ctohb.com/dora): https://www.devops-research.com/quickcheck.html#questions

BOOK REFERENCES

- **Netflix Keeper Test** (ctohb.com/keeper): https://empowerment.ee/wp-content/uploads/2021/05/NETFLIX-%E2%80%93-THE-KEEPER-TEST.pdf

- **Why GitLab Pays Local Rates** (ctohb.com/local): https://about.gitlab.com/blog/2019/02/28/why-we-pay-local-rates/

- **What is the topgrading interview process?** (ctohb.com/interview): https://www.greenhouse.io/blog/what-is-the-topgrading-interview-process

- **Topgrading** (ctohb.com/topgrading): https://en.wikipedia.org/wiki/Topgrading

- **Painting the Bridge** (ctohb.com/painting): https://www.goldengate.org/bridge/bridge-maintenance/painting-the-bridge/

- **Dare to Lead: The BRAVING Inventory** (ctohb.com/braving): https://brenebrown.com/resources/the-braving-inventory/

- **Root Cause Analysis Template** (ctohb.com/rca): https://docs.google.com/document/d/1GuRZgDpMVg_Qf3sR7r8tZqRx6Re0oBrwIcnj-ekgJ60/edit#

- **Ship Small Diffs** (ctohb.com/diffs): https://blog.skyliner.io/ship-small-diffs-741308bec0d1

- **GitHub Flow, Trunk-Based Development, and Code Reviews** (ctohb.com/branching): https://reviewpad.com/blog/github-flow-trunk-based-development-and-code-reviews

- **Ship/Show/Ask** (ctohb.com/ssa): https://martinfowler.com/articles/ship-show-ask.html

- **Thoughtworks Technology Radar 27** (ctohb.com/techradar): https://www.thoughtworks.com/en-us/radar

- **Feature Toggles (aka Feature Flags)** (ctohb.com/hodgson): https://martinfowler.com/articles/feature-toggles.html

- **Multi-stage Builds** (ctohb.com/docker): https://docs.docker.com/build/building/multi-stage/

BOOK REFERENCES

- **Choose Boring Technology** (ctohb.com/boring): https://boringtechnology.club/

- **Technology Radar** (ctohb.com/radar): https://www.thoughtworks.com/en-us/radar

- **The Waterfall Model** (ctohb.com/waterfall): https://en.wikipedia.org/wiki/Waterfall_model#History

- **The Pragmatic Programmer** (ctohb.com/tpp): https://en.wikipedia.org/wiki/The_Pragmatic_Programmer

- **Rubber Duck Debugging** (ctohb.com/rdd): https://en.wikipedia.org/wiki/Rubber_duck_debugging

- **FrequencyReducesDifficulty** (ctohb.com/fowler): https://martinfowler.com/bliki/FrequencyReducesDifficulty.html

- **Figma Material Design** (ctohb.com/figma): https://www.figma.com/@materialdesign

- **How to Design with the Atlassian Design System** (ctohb.com/design): https://atlassian.design/get-started/design

- **Building Productive Teams** (ctohb.com/teams): https://docs.microsoft.com/en-us/DevOps/plan/building-productive-teams

- **GitHub Compensation Calculator** (ctohb.com/calc): https://about.gitlab.com/handbook/total-rewards/compensation/

- **Codeacademy Engineering Competencies** (ctohb.com/competencies): https://github.com/Codecademy/engineering-competencies

- **The Multitasking Myth** (ctohb.com/myth): https://blog.codinghorror.com/the-multi-tasking-myth

- **Acronyms Seriously Suck: Elon Musk** (ctohb.com/acronyms): https://gist.github.com/klaaspieter/12cd68f54bb71a3940eae5cdd4ea1764

- **How We Work Without Meetings at Levels** (ctohb.com/async): https://medium.com/levelshealth/how-we-work-without-meetings-at-levels-a6a525e21aa5

- **Collaborate with kindness: Consider these etiquette tips in**

**Slack** (ctohb.com/slack): https://slack.com/blog/collaboration/etiquette-tips-in-slack

- **How to Use Skip-Level Meetings Effectively** (ctohb.com/skip): https://www.managementcenter.org/resources/skip-level-meeting-toolkit/

- **From Founder to CTO** (ctohb.com/founder2cto): https://calv.info/founder-cto

- **How to Prioritize the Developer Experience and Improve Output** (ctohb.com/dx): https://www.harness.io/blog/developer-experience

# 6

# GLOSSARY

- **Agile ceremony**: Agile ceremonies are meetings where a development team comes together at various stages during the development process for discussions on planning future work, communicating ongoing work or reviewing and reflecting on past work.

- **Applicant Tracking System (ATS)**: An applicant tracking system (ATS) is software for recruiters and employers to track candidates throughout the recruiting and hiring process.

- **Boy Scout Rule**: Leave things better than you found them. As applied to a technical team, whenever you work in an area of code, always make even a small improvement, maybe to tests, or documentation, or otherwise improve clarity, readability or maintainability.

- **Brownfield development**: The opposite of greenfield development: working with existing legacy systems, often heavily impacted by tech debt. You're stuck with the high-level decisions that have been made in the past and you have limited flexibility for large change.

- **Business Intelligence (BI)**: Business intelligence (BI) is software that ingests business data and presents it in user-friendly views such as reports, dashboards, charts and graphs.

- **ClickOps**: ClickOps is the error-prone and time-consuming process of having people click-through various menu options in cloud providers'

GLOSSARY

websites, to select and configure the correct automated computing infrastructure.

- **Containerization**: Containerization involves packaging software that contains all the necessary elements to run an application into a container environment. This allows organizations to run applications from anywhere - in a private datacenter, public cloud or even a personal laptop.

- **Context switching**: Changing from one task to another. For engineers that means setting aside the problem being worked on and starting to work on another. The act of switching is generally time consuming and less efficient than working on one problem at a time.

- **Direct report**: Direct reports are employees who report directly to someone who is above them in the organization chart, often a manager, supervisor, or team leader.

- **Engineering Product and Design (EPD)**: The idea of combining together into a single department what traditionally has been three separate departments: Design, Product and Engineering. The order of the acronym is often changed, EDP, PDE.

- **Greenfield solution**: Greenfield software development refers to development work in a new environment with minimal pre-existing legacy code and free choice on tools, patterns, and architecture.

- **Horizon One/Two/Three**: Each horizon represents a different time scale. Horizon one is generally short term (days/weeks), two is medium (months) and three long term (years). Often used as a planning tool to ensure you're accommodating each horizon.

- **Idempotent**: A technical operation is idempotent if subsequent executions of the operation do not change the output.

- **Kaizen**: Kaizen is the philosophy of continuously improving all processes in an organization.

- **Key Performance Indicator (KPI)**: KPIs are the critical quantifiable indicators of progress toward an intended result. Sometimes referred to as "input metrics."

GLOSSARY

- **Objectives and Key Results (OKRs)**: Objectives and key results is a goal-setting framework, originating at Intel in the 1970s, used by individuals, teams, and organizations to define measurable goals and track their outcomes.

- **Pigeonhole principle**: Describes a circumstance where there is a fixed number of outcomes and a larger number of trials. If you flip a coin three times then at least one of heads or tails must come up twice.

- **Product Requirements Document (PRD)**: A PRD is a document that gathers into one place the background, references, justification for and articulation of the requirements for a product.

- **Reproducibility**: The ability to reproduce a given outcome on demand. Generally in software development it takes the form of "a user pushes button X, then the application crashes." If pushing the button is a complete and reliable description of how to cause the application crash then this is a reproducible crash with understood reproduction steps.

- **Request for Comment (RFC)**: A document that outlines an idea, philosophy, proposal or methodology that is intended to collect feedback and ultimately become a long-lived reference material.

- **Root Cause Analysis (RCA)**: An approach, and generally a document, that attempts to dig below the superficial to truly understand why an event occurred. Generally used as an investigative tool, and then reference documentation, for why an incident occurred in a software project.

- **SaaS Management Platform (SMP)**: A SMP provides a single location to review, manage, optimize and govern SaaS tools used across an organization.

- **Service-Oriented Architecture (SOA)**: The phrase Service-Oriented Architecture (SOA) originated in the 1990s and is used to refer to some fairly specific technology choices. Nowadays, the phrase is used to more broadly describe a system where information moves between parts of the system over a network

GLOSSARY

- **Standup meeting**: (aka "Daily Scrum") A regular meeting as part of the scrum/agile ceremonies. Generally intended to be short, less than 30 minutes, to facilitate communication, updates, conflict resolution and decision making within a team.

- **Straw Man Model**: A first draft proposition that can be put together rapidly with incomplete data. Often used as a starting place proposal with a team to accelerate the process of collecting feedback and getting to a solution.

- **Synchronous/Asynchronous Workplace Culture**: The idea of an asynchronous workplace culture is that communication flows are encouraged to asynchronously, that is, without needing both sides of the communication to participate at the same time. For example, a written document facilitates asynchronous communication, the author need not be present when the readers consume the document. Asynchronous cultures de-emphasize meetings and emphasize written or recorded audio/video documentation.

# ABOUT THE AUTHOR

Zach Goldberg graduated from the University of Pennsylvania magna cum laude with a degree in Computer Science and Engineering. He's been the CTO of six startups including WiFast, Sticks and Brains, AutoLotto, Trellis Technologies, GrowFlow (acq. Dama Financial, 2022), and Towards Equilibrium Inc, as well as an Entrepreneur-in-Residence at Tencent and an Associate Product Manager at Google. After Dama acquired GrowFlow in 2022, Zach sat down and poured all of his experience into this book. Learn more about Zach's work at zachgoldberg.com.

# ABOUT THE PUBLISHER

Founded in 2021 by Bryna Haynes, WorldChangers Media is a boutique publishing company focused on "Ideas for Impact." We know that great books change lives, topple outdated paradigms, and build movements. Our commitment is to deliver superior-quality transformational nonfiction by, and for, the next generation of thought leaders.

Ready to write and publish your thought leadership book with us? Learn more at www.WorldChangers.Media.

Made in the USA
Middletown, DE
09 July 2024